FOLENS FRENCH VERBS

Regular and Irregular

by

Hilda O'Sullivan, B.A., H.D.E.

FOLENS

TABLE OF CONTENTS

INTRODUCTORY NOTE

Students ought to learn the verbs marked with two asterisks, **, first; then those marked with one asterisk,*. All the verbs marked with one or two asterisks form part and parcel of basic French, *le Français fondamental.* Most of them are regular, i.e. they are conjugated like **donner, finir,** or **vendre.** The irregular ones need special study.

The verbs without asterisks, all of them irregular, are given here for the benefit of advanced students and for reference purposes.

Many verbs on our list at the back of the book are also conjugated as reflexive verbs, e.g. **abaisser, s'abaisser.** It should be clearly understood that while both verbs have the same conjugational endings as **donner,** the first, **abaisser,** is conjugated with **avoir,** e.g. **elle a abaissé le montant de la facture,** *she reduced the amount on the invoice,* while the second, **s'abaisser,** though having the same endings as **abaisser** (and therefore as **donner**) is conjugated with **être,** because it is a reflexive verb, e.g. **elle s'est abaissée jusqu'à dire des mensonges,** *she stooped so low as to tell lies.*

A. FORMATION OF TENSES AND MOODS

Le présent de l'indicatif

Also called **le présent,** the Present, or the Present Indicative. We must be aware of the fact that the English tenses and moods do not correspond exactly to their so-called equivalents in French. This is why we often use the French names.

About 4,000 verbs ending in **-er** in the Infinitive are conjugated like **donner;** about 300 verbs ending in **-ir** are conjugated like **finir,** and about 50 ending in **-re** are conjugated like **vendre.** They form the three classes of regular conjugations.

The **-er** and **-ir** conjugations are live conjugations, i.e. all newly created verbs are formed on the model of one of them, e.g. **radiographier,** *to take an x-ray,* follows the model of **donner; allunir,** *to land on the moon,* follows the model of **finir.**

To conjugate the regular verbs in the Present Indicative we drop the last two letters of their Infinitive and add for the respective three conjugations the endings printed in red.

	Donner		**Finir**		**Vendre**
je	donne, *I give*	je	finis, *I finish*	je	vends, *I sell*
tu	donnes, *you give*	tu	finis, *you finish*	tu	vends, *you sell*
il	donne, *he gives*	il	finit, *he finishes*	il	vend, *he sells*
nous	donnons, *we give*	nous	finissons, *we finish*	nous	vendons, *we sell*
vous	donnez, *you give*	vous	finissez, *you finish*	vous	vendez, *you sell*
ils	donnent, *they give*	ils	finissent, *they finish*	ils	vendent, *they sell*

Nearly all irregular verbs are also irregular in the Present Indicative.

L'imparfait de l'indicatif

Also called **l'imparfait,** or the Imperfect.

To form the Imperfect we take the **nous**-form of the verb in the Present Tense, we drop the **-ons** and add the endings **-ais, -ais, -ait, -ions, -iez, -aient.**

nous	**donnons**	**nous**	**finissons**	**nous**	**prenons**
je	donnais *(a)*	je	finissais	je	prenais
tu	donnais	tu	finissais	tu	prenais
il	donnait	il	finissait	il	prenait
nous	donnions	nous	finissions	nous	prenions
vous	donniez	vous	finissiez	vous	preniez
ils	donnaient	ils	finissaient	ils	prenaient

(a) I was giving, I used to give, I would give (in the sense of *I used to give*), *I gave,* are all correct translations of **je donnais** depending on the context.

Other examples:

nous jetons	je jetais tu jetais il jetait	nous jetions vous jetiez ils jetaient
nous mangeons	je mangeais tu mangeais il mangeait	nous mangions vous mangiez ils mangeaient
nous lançons	je lançais tu lançais il lançait	nous lancions vous lanciez ils lançaient

Note that before **i** there is no **e** after the **g** nor a cedilla under the **c:** nous mangions, vous lanciez.

All the irregular verbs follow this rule with the exception of only one, **être,** *to be* **(nous sommes,** *we are***),** whose Imperfect is **j'étais, tu étais, il était, nous étions, vous étiez, ils étaient.**

Le passé simple

Also called **le passé défini, le passé historique,** the Past Definite, the Past Historic.

The endings of the Past Historic of all the regular verbs in **-er, -ir, -re** are as shown in the following examples.

Donner *I gave*	**Finir** *I finished*	**Vendre** *I sold*
je donnai	je finis	je vendis
tu donnas	tu finis	tu vendis
il donna	il finit	il vendit
nous donnâmes	nous finîmes	nous vendîmes
vous donnâtes	vous finîtes	vous vendîtes
ils donnèrent	ils finirent	ils vendirent

The Past Historic of the irregular verbs is highly irregular but, with the exception of **venir,** *to come*, and **tenir,** *to hold,* they all end in

-is	**-îmes**		**-us**	**-ûmes**
-is	**-îtes**	or	**-us**	**-ûtes**
-it	**-irent**		**-ut**	**-urent**

Le passé composé

1. The **passé composé**, Perfect Tense, of a verb consists of the Present Tense of the verb **avoir** or **être** and the Past Participle.

   (a) The verbs conjugated with **être** are:

   (i) the following twelve: **aller, arriver, descendre, entrer, monter, mourir, naître, partir, rester, sortir, tomber, venir.** E.g. **je suis allé, je suis arrivé.**

   (ii) all the reflexive verbs. See page 15.

   (b) All the other verbs are conjugated with **avoir.**

2. Some verbs, of which the most important ones are **accourir, disparaître, échapper, passer** are conjugated with **avoir** when denoting action, with **être** when denoting a state. It is often difficult to decide which auxiliary is to be used.

Elle a disparu derrière ce coin de rue.	*She disappeared behind that street corner.*
Elle est disparue.	*She is gone. She has disappeared.*

3. **Descendre, entrer, monter,** and **sortir** are usually conjugated with **être** but they are conjugated with **avoir** when they have a Direct Object. This applies also to their compounds **rentrer, remonter,** etc.

Elle est montée dans sa chambre.	*She went up to her room.*
Elle a monté l'escalier.	*She mounted the stairs.*
Elle a monté ses bagages.	*She carried her luggage upstairs.*

4. **Retourner** is conjugated
   with **avoir** when it means *to send back, give back, turn round something* or *turn up something,*
   with **être** when it means *to go back.*

Le participe passé

1. Regular Verbs.
   The Past Participle of regular verbs in

-er ends in é	**donner, j'ai donné; aller, je suis allé**
-ir ends in **i**	**finir, j'ai fini**
-re ends in **u**	**vendre, j'ai vendu** **descendre, je suis descendu**

2. Irregular Verbs.
   The Past Participle of the irregular verbs has to be learnt off by heart.

Agreement of the Past Participle

1. A Past Participle used with **être** agrees with the Subject.

Ma sœur est allée à l'école. — *My sister has gone to school.*

2. A Past Participle used with **avoir** agrees with the Preceding Direct Object.

Elle a pris les lettres et les a mises à la poste. — *She took the letters and posted them.*

3. The Past Participle of a reflexive verb, like that used with **avoir,** agrees with the Preceding Direct Object.

Elle s'est lavée. — *She washed herself.*

Elle s'est lavé les mains. — *She washed her hands.*

Elles se sont saluées. — *They greeted one another.*

Elles se sont écrit. — *They wrote to one another.*

4. The Partitive **en,** meaning *some of them, of it, etc.* is not a Direct Object and, consequently, it does not influence the Past Participle.

Avez-vous des pommes? — Oui, j'en ai acheté. — *Have you any apples? – Yes, I bought some.*

5. A Past Participle used without an auxiliary (**être** or **avoir**) agrees, like an adjective, with the noun it qualifies.

Les fillettes, enchantées de ce que la maîtresse n'était pas là, se mirent à rire et à bavarder. — *The girls, delighted that the mistress was not there, started to laugh and to chatter.*

Le participe présent

To form the Present Participle one takes the **nous**-form of the verb in the Present Tense and replaces the **-ons** by **-ant.**

nous finissons, finissant, *finishing*
nous prenons, prenant, *taking*

There are only three exceptions to this rule:

nous sommes, **étant,** *being*
nous avons, **ayant,** *having*
nous savons, **sachant,** *knowing*

Le futur simple

(a) The Future of regular verbs.
To form the Future of a verb one adds

-ai	**-ons**
-as	**-ez**
-a	**-ont**

to its Infinitive, but the verbs ending in **-re** (e.g. **vendre**) drop the final e first.

Donner		**Finir**		**Vendre**	
I shall give		*I shall finish*		*I shall sell*	
je	donnerai	je	finirai	je	vendrai
tu	donneras	tu	finiras	tu	vendras
il	donnera	il	finira	il	vendra
nous	donnerons	nous	finirons	nous	vendrons
vous	donnerez	vous	finirez	vous	vendrez
ils	donneront	ils	finiront	ils	vendront

(b) As for the Future of **-er** verbs with spelling peculiarities in their conjugation, such as **nettoyer, payer, lever, appeler, jeter,** see pages 16 to 20.

(c) There are quite a number of verbs which are irregular in the Future though they all take the same endings as above: **-ai, -as, -a, -ons, -ez, -ont,** e.g. **aller, j'irai,** *I shall go,* **tu iras,** etc.

Le conditionnel

The Conditional of all verbs, regular and irregular, is formed by adding the endings of the Imperfect to the stem of the Future.

Infinitif	**Futur**	**Imparfait**		**Conditionnel**	
				I would give	
Donner	je donnerai	je	donnais	je	donnerais
		tu	donnais	tu	donnerais
		il	donnait	il	donnerait
		nous	donnions	nous	donnerions
		vous	donniez	vous	donneriez
		ils	donnaient	ils	donneraient

More Examples:

Futur	**Conditionnel**	**Futur**	**Conditionnel**
je lèverai	je lèverais	j'irai	j'irais
je paierai	je paierais	j'aurai	j'aurais
or je payerai	or je payerais	je serai	je serais
j'appellerai	j'appellerais		

L'impératif

To form the Imperative of a verb we take its

second person singular, i.e.	tu . . .
first person plural	nous . . .
second person plural	vous . . .

of the Present Tense and we drop the pronouns. But if the Infinitive of the verb ends in **-er** and in the case of other verbs conjugated like those in **-er** (e.g. **ouvrir**), the final **s** of the second person singular is dropped.

Prendre

tu	prends	prends, *take*
nous	prenons	prenons, *let us take*
vous	prenez	prenez, *take*

Donner

tu	donnes	donne
nous	donnons	donnons
vous	donnez	donnez

Aller

tu	vas	va
nous	allons	allons
vous	allez	allez

There are four exceptions to this rule:

Être
sois, *be*
soyons, *let us be*
soyez, *be*

Avoir
aie, *have*
ayons, *let us have*
ayez, *have*

Savoir
sache, *know*
sachons, *let us know*
sachez, *know*

Vouloir
veuille, *be so good as to*
veuillons, *let us*
veuillez, *be so good as to*

Le présent du subjonctif

1. General Rule.

To form the Present Subjunctive of a verb we take the **nous**-form of the Present Indicative, drop the **-ons** and add the endings

-e	**-ions**
-es	**-iez**
-e	**-ent**

Present Indicative	**Present Subjunctive**	
nous donnons	que je donne	que nous donnions
	que tu donnes	que vous donniez
	qu'il donne	qu'ils donnent
nous finissons	que je finisse, etc.	
nous vendons	que je vende, etc.	

2. (a) Many irregular verbs form their Subjunctive quite regularly, e.g.

nous battons	que je batte, etc.
nous disons	que je dise, etc.
nous écrivons	que j'écrive, etc.
nous lisons	que je lise, etc.
nous mettons	que je mette, etc.

(b) Certain verbs in **-er** such as **nettoyer, payer, lever, céder, appeler, jeter,** see pages 17 - 20, undergo certain small changes in their stem when the ending contains a mute **e.**

Present Indicative: **je nettoie, je paie** (or **je paye**), **je lève, je cède, j'appelle, je jette.**

Those changes also occur in the Subjunctive: **que je nettoie,** etc.

3. But most irregular verbs form their Subjunctive irregularly, e.g.

Present Indicative	**Present Subjunctive**
nous allons	que j'aille
nous avons	que j'aie
etc.	etc.

L'imparfait du subjonctif

We form the 1st person of the Imperfect Subjunctive by adding **-se** to the 2nd person singular of the Past Definite **(passé simple).**

The endings of the Imperfect Subjunctive are:

-sse	**-ssions**
-sses	**-ssiez**
-ˆt	**-ssent**

E.g. **Donner** — **Finir** — **Vendre**

Past Definite

Donner		**Finir**		**Vendre**	
tu donnas		**tu finis**		**tu vendis**	
Imperfect Subjunctive					
que je	donnasse	que je	finisse	que je	vendisse
que tu	donnasses	que tu	finisses	que tu	vendisses
qu'il	donnât	qu'il	finît	qu'il	vendît
que nous	donnassions	que nous	finissions	que nous	vendissions
que vous	donnassiez	que vous	finissiez	que vous	vendissiez
qu'ils	donnassent	qu'ils	finissent	qu'ils	vendissent

Avoir		**Être**		**Prendre**	
Past Definite					
tu eus		**tu fus**		**tu pris**	
Imperfect Subjunctive					
que j'	eusse	que je	fusse	que je	prisse
que tu	eusses	que tu	fusses	que tu	prisses
qu'il	eût	qu'il	fût	qu'il	prît
que nous	eussions	que nous	fussions	que nous	prissions
que vous	eussiez	que vous	fussiez	que vous	prissiez
qu'ils	eussent	qu'ils	fussent	qu'ils	prissent

There are no exceptions to this rule.

Compound Tenses

See the Compound Tenses of **donner,** p. 11, **monter,** p. 14, and **se laver,** p. 15.

Summary

(applies fully to all regular verbs, only partly to the irregular ones)

From the ↓	*one derives the* ↓		
Infinitive	Future Conditional	donner	je donner**ai**, etc. je donner**ais**, etc.
Present Indic.	Present Participle Imperfect Indicative Present Subjunctive Imperative	nous donn**ons**	donn**ant** je donn**ais**, etc. que je donn**e**, etc. donn**e**, donn**ons**, etc.
Past Definitive	Imperfect Subjunctive	tu donnas	que je donnasse, etc.
Passé composé	all Compound Tenses	j'ai donné	j'avais donné, etc. j'aurai donné, etc. etc.

B. REGULAR VERBS

The full conjugation of the regular verb

DONNER, *to give*

Indicatif

Présent	**Passé composé**
I give	*I have given*
je donne	j'ai donné
tu donnes	tu as donné
il donne	il a donné
nous donnons	nous avons donné
vous donnez	vous avez donné
ils donnent	ils ont donné

Imparfait	**Plus-que-parfait**
I was giving	*I had given*
je donnais	j'avais donné
tu donnais	tu avais donné
il donnait	il avait donné
nous donnions	nous avions donné
vous donniez	vous aviez donné
ils donnaient	ils avaient donné

Passé simple	**Passé antérieur**
I gave	*I had given*
je donnai	j'eus donné
tu donnas	tu eus donné
il donna	il eut donné
nous donnâmes	nous eûmes donné
vous donnâtes	vous eûtes donné
ils donnèrent	ils eurent donné

Futur simple	**Futur antérieur**
I will give	*I will have given*
je donnerai	j'aurai donné
tu donneras	tu auras donné
il donnera	il aura donné
nous donnerons	nous aurons donné
vous donnerez	vous aurez donné
ils donneront	ils auront donné

Infinitif

Présent	**Passé**
donner	avoir donné
to give	*to have given*

Impératif

Présent	**Passé**
give	*have given*
donne	aie donné
donnons	ayons donné
donnez	ayez donné

Conditionnel

Présent	**Passé**
I would give	*I would have given*
je donnerais	j'aurais donné
tu donnerais	tu aurais donné
il donnerait	il aurait donné
nous donnerions	nous aurions donné
vous donneriez	vous auriez donné
ils donneraient	ils auraient donné

Subjonctif

Présent	**Passé**
that I give	*that I have given*
que je donne	que j'aie donné
que tu donnes	que tu aies donné
qu'il donne	qu'il ait donné
que n. donnions	que n. ayons donné
que v. donniez	que v. ayez donné
qu'ils donnent	qu'ils aient donné

Imparfait	**Plus-que-parfait**
that I gave	*that I had given*
que je donnasse	que j'eusse donné
que tu donnasses	que tu eusses donné
qu'il donnât	qu'il eût donné
que n. donnassions	que n. eussions donné
que v. donnassiez	que v. eussiez donné
qu'ils donnassent	qu'ils eussent donné

Participe

Présent	**Passé**
donnant	donné, *given*
giving	ayant donné
	having given

The full conjugation of the regular verb

**FINIR, *to finish*

Indicatif

Présent		**Passé composé**	
I finish		*I have finished*	
je	finis	j'ai	fini
tu	finis	tu as	fini
il	finit	il a	fini
nous	finissons	nous avons	fini
vous	finissez	vous avez	fini
ils	finissent	ils ont	fini

Imparfait		**Plus-que-parfait**	
I was finishing		*I had finished*	
je	finissais	j'avais	fini
tu	finissais	tu avais	fini
il	finissait	il avait	fini
nous	finissions	nous avions	fini
vous	finissiez	vous aviez	fini
ils	finissaient	ils avaient	fini

Passé simple		**Passé antérieur**	
I finished		*I had finished*	
je	finis	j'eus	fini
tu	finis	tu eus	fini
il	finit	il eut	fini
nous	finîmes	nous eûmes	fini
vous	finîtes	vous eûtes	fini
ils	finirent	ils eurent	fini

Futur simple		**Futur antérieur**	
I will finish		*I will have finished*	
je	finirai	j'aurai	fini
tu	finiras	tu auras	fini
il	finira	il aura	fini
nous	finirons	nous aurons	fini
vous	finirez	vous aurez	fini
ils	finiront	ils auront	fini

Infinitif

Présent	**Passé**
finir	avoir fini
to finish	*to have finished*

Impératif

Présent	**Passé**	
finish	*have finished*	
finis	aie	fini
finissons	ayons	fini
finissez	ayez	fini

Conditionnel

Présent		**Passé**	
I would finish		*I would have finished*	
je	finirais	j'aurais	fini
tu	finirais	tu aurais	fini
il	finirait	il aurait	fini
nous	finirions	nous aurions	fini
vous	finiriez	vous auriez	fini
ils	finiraient	ils auraient	fini

Subjonctif

Présent		**Passé**	
that I finish		*that I have finished*	
que je	finisse	que j'aie	fini
que tu	finisses	que tu aies	fini
qu'il	finisse	qu'il ait	fini
que n.	finissions	que n. ayons	fini
que v.	finissiez	que v. ayez	fini
qu'ils	finissent	qu'ils aient	fini

Imparfait		**Plus-que-parfait**	
that I finished		*that I had finished*	
que je	finisse	que j'eusse	fini
que tu	finisses	que tu eusses	fini
qu'il	finît	qu'il eût	fini
que n.	finissions	que n. eussions	fini
que v.	finissiez	que v. eussiez	fini
qu'ils	finissent	qu'ils eussent	fini

Participe

Présent

finissant
finishing

Passé

fini, *finished*
ayant fini
having finished

The full conjugation of the regular verb

**VENDRE, *to sell*

Indicatif

Présent		Passé composé	
I sell		*I have sold*	
je	vends	j'ai	vendu
tu	vends	tu as	vendu
il	vend	il a	vendu
nous	vendons	nous avons	vendu
vous	vendez	vous avez	vendu
ils	vendent	ils ont	vendu

Imparfait		Plus-que-parfait	
I was selling		*I had sold*	
je	vendais	j'avais	vendu
tu	vendais	tu avais	vendu
il	vendait	il avait	vendu
nous	vendions	nous avions	vendu
vous	vendiez	vous aviez	vendu
ils	vendaient	ils avaient	vendu

Passé simple		Passé antérieur	
I sold		*I had sold*	
je	vendis	j'eus	vendu
tu	vendis	tu eus	vendu
il	vendit	il eut	vendu
nous	vendîmes	nous eûmes	vendu
vous	vendîtes	vous eûtes	vendu
ils	vendirent	ils eurent	vendu

Futur simple		Futur antérieur	
I will sell		*I will have sold*	
je	vendrai	j'aurai	vendu
tu	vendras	tu auras	vendu
il	vendra	il aura	vendu
nous	vendrons	nous aurons	vendu
vous	vendrez	vous aurez	vendu
ils	vendront	ils auront	vendu

Infinitif

Présent	Passé
vendre	avoir vendu
to sell	*to have sold*

Impératif

Présent	Passé	
sell	*have sold*	
vends	aie	vendu
vendons	ayons	vendu
vendez	ayez	vendu

Conditionnel

Présent		Passé	
I would sell		*I would have sold*	
je	vendrais	j'aurais	vendu
tu	vendrais	tu aurais	vendu
il	vendrait	il aurait	vendu
nous	vendrions	nous aurions	vendu
vous	vendriez	vous auriez	vendu
ils	vendraient	ils auraient	vendu

Subjonctif

Présent		Passé	
that I sell		*that I have sold*	
que je	vende	que j'aie	vendu
que tu	vendes	que tu aies	vendu
qu'il	vende	qu'il ait	vendu
que n.	vendions	que n. ayons	vendu
que v.	vendiez	que v. ayez	vendu
qu'ils	vendent	qu'ils aient	vendu

Imparfait		Plus-que-parfait	
that I sold		*that I had sold*	
que je	vendisse	que j'eusse	vendu
que tu	vendisses	que tu eusses	vendu
qu'il	vendît	qu'il eût	vendu
que n.	vendissions	que n. eussions	vendu
que v.	vendissiez	que v. eussiez	vendu
qu'ils	vendissent	qu'ils eussent	vendu

Participe

Présent	Passé
vendant	vendu, *sold*
selling	ayant vendu
	having sold

The full conjugation of a regular verb conjugated with **être**

**MONTER, *to climb, to ascend*

Indicatif

Présent	**Passé composé**
I climb	*I have climbed*
je monte	je suis monté
tu montes	tu es monté
il monte	il est monté
nous montons	nous sommes montés
vous montez	vous êtes montés
ils montent	ils sont montés

Imparfait	**Plus-que-parfait**
I was climbing	*I had climbed*
je montais	j'étais monté
tu montais	tu étais monté
il montait	il était monté
nous montions	nous étions montés
vous montiez	vous étiez montés
ils montaient	ils étaient montés

Passé simple	**Passé antérieur**
I climbed	*I had climbed*
je montai	je fus monté
tu montas	je fus monté
il monta	il fut monté
nous montâmes	nous fûmes montés
vous montâtes	vous fûtes montés
ils montèrent	ils furent montés

Futur simple	**Futur antérieur**
I will climb	*I will have climbed*
je monterai	je serai monté
tu monteras	tu seras monté
il montera	il sera monté
nous monterons	nous serons montés
vous monterez	vous serez montés
ils monteront	ils seront montés

Infinitif

Présent	**Passé**
monter	être monté
to climb	*having climbed*

Impératif

Présent	**Passé**
climb	*have climbed*
monte	sois monté
montons	soyons montés
montez	soyez montés

Conditionnel

Présent	**Passé**
I would climb	*I would have climbed*
je monterais	je serais monté
tu monterais	tu serais monté
il monterait	il serait monté
nous monterions	nous serions montés
vous monteriez	vous seriez montés
ils monteraient	ils seraient montés

Subjonctif

Présent	**Passé**
that I climb	*that I have climbed*
que je monte	que je sois monté
que tu montes	que tu sois monté
qu'il monte	qu'il soit monté
que n. montions	que n. soyons montés
que v. montiez	que v. soyez montés
qu'ils montent	qu'ils soient montés

Imparfait	**Plus-que-parfait**
that I climbed	*that I had climbed*
que je montasse	que je fusse monté
que tu montasses	que tu fusse monté
qu'il montât	qu'il fût monté
que n. montassions	que n. fussions montés
que v. montassiez	que v. fussiez montés
qu'ils montassent	qu'ils fussent montés

Participe

Présent	**passé**
montant	monté, *climbed*
climbing	étant monté
	having climbed

The full conjugation of a regular reflexive verb.

**SE LAVER, *to wash oneself*

Indicatif

Présent		**Passé composé**	
I wash myself		*I have washed myself*	
je me	lave	je me suis	lavé
tu te	laves	tu t'es	lavé
il se	lave	il s'est	lavé
n.n.	lavons	n.n. sommes	lavés
v.v.	lavez	v.v. êtes	lavés
ils se	lavent	ils se sont	lavés

Imparfait		**Plus-que-parfait**	
I was washing mys.		*I had washed myself*	
je me	lavais	je m'étais	lavé
tu te	lavais	tu t'étais	lavé
il se	lavait	il s'était	lavé
n.n.	lavions	n.n. étions	lavés
v.v.	laviez	v.v. étiez	lavés
ils se	lavaient	ils s'étaient	lavés

Passé simple		**Passé antérieur**	
I washing myself		*I had washed myself*	
je me	lavai	je me fus	lavé
tu te	lavas	tu te fus	lavé
il se	lava	il se fut	lavé
n.n.	lavâmes	n.n. fûmes	lavés
v.v.	lavâtes	v.v. fûtes	lavés
ils se	lavèrent	ils se furent	lavés

Futur simple		**Futur antérieur**	
I will wash myself		*I will have washed mys.*	
je me	laverai	je me serai	lavé
tu te	laveras	tu te seras	lavé
il se	lavera	il se sera	lavé
n.n.	laverons	n.n. serons	lavés
v.v.	laverez	v.v. serez	lavés
ils se	laveront	ils se seront	lavés

Infinitif

Présent	**Passé**
to wash oneself	*to have washed oneself*
se laver	s'être lavé

Impératif

Présent	**Passé**
wash myself	
lave-toi	*(a)*
lavons-nous	
lavez-vous	

Conditionnel

Présent		**Passé**	
I would wash myself		*I would have washed myself*	
je me	laverais	je me serais	lavé
tu te	laverais	tu te serais	lavé
il se	laverait	il se serait	lavé
n.n.	laverions	n.n. serions	lavés
v.v.	laveriez	v.v. seriez	lavés
ils se	laveraient	ils se seraient	lavés

Subjonctif

Présent		**Passé**	
that I wash myself		*that I had washed myself*	
que je me	lave	que je me sois	lavé
que tu te	laves	que tu te sois	lavé
qu'il se	lave	qu'il se soit	lavé
que n.n.	lavions	que n.n. soyons	lavés
que v.v.	laviez	que v.v. soyez	lavés
qu'ils se	lavent	qu'ils se soient	lavés

Imparfait		**Plus-que-parfait**	
that I washed myself		*that I had washed myself*	
que je me	lavasse	que je me fusse	lavé
que tu te	lavasses	que tu te fusses	lavé
qu'il se	lavât	qu'il se fût	lavé
que n.n.	lavassions	que n.n. fussions	lavés
que v.v.	lavassiez	que v.v. fussiez	lavés
qu'ils se	lavassent	qu'ils se fussent	lavés

Participe

Présent	**Passé**
washing oneself	*having washed oneself*
se lavant	s'étant lavé

(a) The gap means that the verb is not used in that tense or person.

Regular Verbs in -**er** with spelling peculiarities.

Verbs whose Infinitive ends in -**cer** take a cedilla under the **c** before **a** and **o**, otherwise they are conjugated exactly like **donner**.

**PLACER, *to put*

Prés. de l'ind. *I put*	Imparfait *I was putting*	Passé simple *I put*	Futur simple *I will put*
je place	je plaçais	je plaçai	je placerai
tu places	tu plaçais	tu plaças	tu placeras
il place	il plaçait	il plaça	il placera
nous plaçons	nous placions	nous plaçâmes	nous placerons
vous placez	vous placiez	vous plaçâtes	vous placerez
ils placent	ils plaçaient	ils placèrent	ils placeront

Passé composé: j'ai placé . . . elle a placé, *she put, she has put.*

Participe présent: plaçant, *putting.*

Conditionnel *I would put*	Impératif *put*	Prés. du subj. *that I put*	Imparf. du subj. *that I put*
je placerais		que je place	que je plaçasse
tu placerais	place	que tu places	que tu plaçasses
il placerait		qu'il place	qu'il plaçât
nous placerions	plaçons	que n. placions	que n. plaçassions
vous placeriez	placez	que v. placiez	que v. plaçassiez
ils placeraient		qu'ils placent	qu'ils plaçassent

Other common verbs conjugated like **placer** are: ***commencer**, *to start;* ***déplacer**, *to display, to shift;* ***divorcer**, *to divorce;* ***effacer**, *to wipe out;* ***enfoncer**, *to beat in;* ***exercer**, *to train, to exercise;* ***se fiancer**, *to become engaged;* ***lancer**, *to throw;* ***menacer**, *to threaten;* ***prononcer**, *to pronounce;* ***remplacer**, *to replace.*

Verbs whose Infinitive ends in -**ger** take an **e** after the **g** before **a** and **o**, otherwise they are conjugated exactly like **donner**.

**MANGER, *to eat*

Prés. de l'ind. *I eat*	Imparfait *I was eating*	Passé simple *I ate*	Futur simple *I will eat*
je mange	je mangeais	je mangeai	je mangerai
tu manges	tu mangeais	tu mangeas	tu mangeras
il mange	il mangeait	il mangea	il mangera
nous mangeons	nous mangions	nous mangeâmes	nous mangerons
vous mangez	vous mangiez	vous mangeâtes	vous mangerez
ils mangent	ils mangeaient	ils mangèrent	ils mangeront

Passé composé: j'ai mangé . . . elle a mangé, *she ate, she has eaten*			
Participe présent: mangeant, *eating*			
Conditionnel *I would eat* je mangerais tu mangerais il mangerait nous mangerions vous mangeriez ils mangeraient	**Impératif** *eat* mange mangeons mangez	**Prés. du subj.** *that I eat* que je mange que tu manges qu'il mange que n. mangions que v. mangiez qu'ils mangent	**Imparf. du subj.** *that I ate* que je mangeasse que tu mangeasses qu'il mangeât que n. mangeassions que v. mangeassiez qu'ils mangeassent

Other common verbs which are conjugated like **manger** are: ***bouger,** *to move;* ***changer,** *to change;* ***charger,** *to load;* ***décharger,** *to unload;* ***déménager,** *to move house;* ***déranger,** *to disturb;* ***diriger,** *to direct;* ***échanger,** *to exchange;* ***engager,** *to engage;* ***exiger,** *to demand;* ***interroger,** *to question;* ***mélanger,** *to mix;* ***plonger,** *to dive, to plunge;* ***ranger,** *to put in order;* ***voyager,** *to travel.*

Verbs whose Infinitive ends in **-oyer** or **-uyer** change the **y** into **i** before an **e** mute (in the endings **-e, -es, -ent, -erai, . . ., -erais, . . .**).

**NETTOYER, *to clean*

Prés. de l'ind. *I clean*	**Imparfait** *I was cleaning*	**Passé simple** *I cleaned*	**Futur simple** *I will clean*
je nettoie tu nettoies il nettoie nous nettoyons vous nettoyez ils nettoient	je nettoyais tu nettoyais il nettoyait nous nettoyions vous nettoyiez ils nettoyaient	je nettoyai tu nettoyas il nettoya nous nettoyâmes vous nettoyâtes ils nettoyèrent	je nettoierai tu nettoieras il nettoiera nous nettoierons vous nettoierez ils nettoieront
Passé composé: j'ai nettoyé . . . elle a nettoyé, *she cleaned, she has cleaned*			
Participe présent: nettoyant, *cleaning*			
Conditionnel *I would clean* je nettoierais tu nettoierais il nettoierait nous nettoierions vous nettoieriez ils nettoieraient	**Impératif** *clean* nettoie nettoyons nettoyez	**Prés. du subj.** *that I clean* que je nettoie que tu nettoies qu'il nettoie que n. nettoyions que v. nettoyiez qu'ils nettoient	**Imparf. du subj.** *that I cleaned* que je nettoyasse que tu nettoyasses qu'il nettoyât que n. nettoyassions que v. nettoyassiez qu'ils nettoyassent

Other common verbs conjugated like **nettoyer** are: ***employer,** *to use,* and ***noyer,** *to drown.* Common verbs in **-uyer** are ***essuyer,** *to wipe,* and ***appuyer,** *to lean on.* ***Envoyer,** *to send,* (see p. 33) and ***renvoyer,** *to send back,* however, are irregular in the Future and the Conditional.

Verbs in **-ayer** may: (a) keep the **y** throughout the whole conjugation or (b) replace the **y** by an **i** before **e** mute, i.e. before the endings **-e, -es, -ent, -erai, -erais . . .**; e.g. **je paye** (pronounce pèy) or **je paie** (pronounce pé). If one follows (b) the conjugation runs as below.

**PAYER, *to pay*

Prés. de l'ind. *I pay*	**Imparfait** *I was paying*	**Passé simple** *I paid*	**Futur simple** *I will pay*
je paie	je payais	je payai	je paierai
tu paies	tu payais	tu payas	tu paieras
il paie	il payait	il paya	il paiera
nous payons	nous payions	nous payâmes	nous paierons
vous payez	vous payiez	vous payâtes	vous paierez
ils payaient	ils payaient	ils payèrent	ils paieront

Passé composé: j'ai payé . . . elle a payé, *she paid, she has paid.*

Participe présent: payant, *paying.*

Conditionnel *I would pay*	**Impératif** *pay*	**Prés. du subj.** *that I pay*	**Imparf. du subj.** *that I paid*
je paierais		que je paie	que je payasse
tu paierais	paie	que tu paies	que tu payasses
il paierait		qu'il paie	qu'il payât
nous paierions	payons	que n. payions	que n. payassions
vous paieriez	payez	que v. payiez	que v. payassiez
ils paieraient		qu'ils paient	qu'ils payassent

Other common verbs which are conjugated like **payer** are: ***balayer,** *to sweep;* ***effrayer,** *to frighten;* ***essayer,** *to try.*

Verbs, whose Infinitive has an **e** mute in its second last syllable, change the **e** mute into **è** if followed by a mute syllable.

**LEVER, *to raise, to lift (up)*

Prés. de l'ind. *I raise*	**Imparfait** *I was raising*	**Passé simple** *I raised*	**Futur simple** *I will raise*
je lève	je levais	je levai	je lèverai
tu lèves	tu levais	tu levas	tu lèveras
il lève	il levait	il leva	il lèvera
nous levons	nous levions	nous levâmes	nous lèverons
vous levez	vous leviez	vous levâtes	vous lèverez
ils lèvent	ils levaient	ils levèrent	ils lèveront

Passé composé: j'ai levé . . . elle a levé, *she raised, she has raised.*

Participe présent: levant, *raising.*

Conditionnel *I would raise*	Impératif *raise*	Prés. du subj. *that I raise*	Imparf. du subj. *that I raised*
je lèverais		que je lève	que je levasse
tu lèverais	lève	que tu lèves	que tu levasses
il lèverait		qu'il lève	qu'il levât
nous lèverions	levons	que n. levions	que n. levassions
vous lèveriez	levez	que v. leviez	que v. levassiez
ils lèveraient		qu'ils lèvent	qu'ils levassent

Other common verbs conjugated like **lever** are: ***acheter,** *to buy;* ***amener,** *to bring, to lead (hither);* ***crever,** *to burst, to die (of animals);* ***élever,** *to raise, to bring up;* ***emmener,** *to lead, to take (s.o.) away;* ***enlever,** *to remove, to carry off;* ***geler,** *to freeze;* ***mener,** *to lead;* **peser,** *to weigh;* ***relever,** *to raise up again;* ***soulever,** *to raise with an effort.*

Verbs whose second last syllable of the Infinitive has an **é**, change the **é** into **è** before a final mute syllable (the **de** in **je céderai** is mute, but not final, but it is mute and final in **il cède**).

**CÉDER, *to give in, to yield*

Prés. de l'ind. *I give in*	Imparfait *I was giving in*	Passé simple *I gave in*	Futur simple *I will give in*
je cède	je cédais	je cédai	je céderai
tu cèdes	tu cédais	tu cédas	tu céderas
il cède	il cédait	il céda	il cédera
nous cédons	nous cédions	nous cédâmes	nous céderons
vous cédez	vous cédiez	vous cédâtes	vous céderez
ils cèdent	ils cédaient	ils cédèrent	ils céderont

Passé composé: j'ai cédé . . . elle a **cédé,** *she gave in, she has given in.*

Participe présent: cédant, *giving in.*

Conditionnel *I would give in*	Impératif *give in*	Prés. du subj. *that I give in*	Imparf. du subj. *that I gave in*
je céderais		que je cède	que je cédasse
tu céderais	cède	que tu cèdes	que tu cédasses
il céderait		qu'il cède	qu'il cédât
nous céderions	cédons	que n. cédions	que n. cédassions
vous céderiez	cédez	que v. cédiez	que v. cédassiez
ils céderaient		qu'ils cèdent	qu'ils cédassent

Common verbs conjugated like **céder** are: ***désespérer,** *to despair;* ***espérer,** *to hope;* ***posséder,** *to possess;* ***préférer,** *to prefer;* **procéder,** *to proceed;* ***protéger,** *to protect;* **répéter,** *to repeat;* ***révéler,** *to reveal, to disclose.*

Appeler and **jeter**, though their second last syllable has an **e** mute, do not follow the same conjugation as **lever**. They double their **l** and **t** if followed by a mute syllable.

**APPELER, *to call*

Prés. de l'ind. *I call*	Imparfait *I was calling*	Passé simple *I called*	Futur simple *I will call*
j' appelle	j' appelais	j' appelai	j' appellerai
tu appelles	tu appelais	tu appelas	tu appelleras
il appelle	il appelait	il appela	il appellera
nous appelons	nous appelions	nous appelâmes	nous appellerons
vous appelez	vous appeliez	vous appelâtes	vous appellerez
ils appellent	ils appelaient	ils appelèrent	ils appelleront

Passé composé: j'ai appelé . . . elle a appelé, *she called, she has called.*

Participe présent: appelant, *calling.*

Conditionnel *I would call*	Impératif *call*	Prés. du subj. *that I call*	Imparf. du subj. *that I called*
j' appellerais		que j' appelle	que j' appelasse
tu appellerais	appelle	que tu appelles	que tu appelasses
il appellerait		qu'il appelle	qu'il appelât
nous appellerions	appelons	que n. appelions	que n. appelassions
vous appelleriez	appelez	que v. appeliez	que v. appelassiez
ils appelleraient		qu'ils appellent	qu'ils appelassent

***Rappeler,** *to call back,* is conjugated like **appeler.**

**JETER, *to throw*

Prés. de l'ind. *I throw*	Imparfait *I was throwing*	Passé simple *I threw*	Futur simple *I will throw*
je jette	je jetais	je jetai	je jetterai
tu jettes	tu jetais	tu jetas	tu jetteras
il jette	il jetait	il jeta	il jettera
nous jetons	nous jetions	nous jetâmes	nous jetterons
vous jetez	vous jetiez	vous jetâtes	vous jetterez
ils jettent	ils jetaient	ils jetèrent	ils jetteront

Passé composé: j'ai jeté . . . elle a jeté, *she threw, she has thrown.*

Participe présent: jetant, *throwing.*

Conditionnel *I would throw*	Impératif *throw*	Prés. du subj. *that I throw*	Imparf. du subj. *(that) I threw*
je jetterais		que je jette	que je jetasse
tu jetterais	jette	que tu jettes	que tu jetasses
il jetterait		qu'il jette	qu'il jetât
nous jetterions	jetons	que n. jetions	que n. jetassions
vous jetteriez	jetez	que v. jetiez	que v. jetassiez
ils jetteraient		qu'ils jettent	qu'ils jetassent

Rejeter, *to reject,* is conjugated like **jeter.**

C. IRREGULAR VERBS

ACQUÉRIR, *to acquire, to obtain*

Prés. de l'ind. *I acquire*	**Imparfait** *I was acquiring*	**Passé simple** *I acquired*	**Futur simple** *I will acquire*
j' acquiers	j' acquérais	j' acquis	j' acquerrai
tu acquiers	tu acquérais	tu acquis	tu acquerras
il acquiert	il acquérait	il acquit	il acquerra
nous acquérons	nous acquérions	nous acquîmes	nous acquerrons
vous acquérez	vous acquériez	vous acquîtes	vous acquerrez
ils acquièrent	ils acquéraient	ils acquirent	ils acquerront

Passé composé: j'ai acquis . . . elle a acquis, *she acquired, she has acquired.*

Participe présent: acquérant, *acquiring, obtaining.*

Conditionnel *I would acquire*	**Impératif** *acquire*	**Prés. du subj.** *that I acquire*	**Imparf. du subj.** *that I acquired*
j' acquerrais		que j' acquière	que j' acquisse
tu acquerrais	acquiers	que tu acquières	que tu acquisses
il acquerrait		qu'il acquière	qu'il acquît
nous acquerrions	acquérons	que n. acquérions	que n. acquissions
vous acquerriez	acquérez	que v. acquériez	que v. acquissiez
ils acquerraient		qu'ils acquièrent	qu'ils acquissent

Conquérir, *to conquer;* **s'enquérir,** *to inquire;* **quérir,** *to fetch;* **reconquérir,** *to regain;* **requérir,** *to demand, to ask for,* are conjugated like **acquérir.**

**ALLER, *to go*

Prés. de l'ind. *I go*	**Imparfait** *I was going*	**Passé simple** *I went*	**Futur simple** *I will go*
je vais	j' allais	j' allai	j' irai
tu vas	tu allais	tu allas	tu iras
il va	il allait	il alla	il ira
nous allons	nous allions	nous allâmes	nous irons
vous allez	vous alliez	vous allâtes	vous irez
ils vont	ils allaient	ils allèrent	ils iront

Passé composé: je suis allé . . . elle est allée, *she went, she has gone.*

Participe présent: allant, *going.*

Conditionnel *I would go*	**Impératif** *go*	**Prés. du subj.** *that I go*	**Imparf. du subj.** *that I went*
j' irais		que j' aille	que j' allasse
tu irais	va	que tu ailles	que tu allasses
il irait		qu'il aille	qu'il allât
nous irions	allons	que n. allions	que n. allassions
vous iriez	allez	que v. alliez	que v. allassiez
ils iraient		qu'ils aillent	qu'ils allassent

N.B. In the Imperative **va** becomes **vas** before **y: vas-y.** Note the **t** in **va-t-il? S'en aller,** *to go away,* is conjugated like **aller.** Note the position of **en** in **je m'en suis**

allé (not **je me suis en allé**) and the **t'** instead of **te** in **va-t'en. S'en aller** is conjugated with the help of **être** in the compound tenses.

ASSAILLIR, *to assail, to attack, to assault*

Prés. de l'ind. *I attack*	**Imparfait** *I was attacking*	**Passé simple** *I attacked*	**Futur simple** *I will attack*
j' assaille	j' assaillais	j' assaillis	j' assaillirai
tu assailles	tu assaillais	tu assaillis	tu assailliras
il assaille	il assaillait	il assaillit	il assaillira
nous assaillons	nous assaillions	nous assaillîmes	nous assaillirons
vous assaillez	vous assailliez	vous assaillîtes	vous assaillirez
ils assaillent	ils assaillaient	ils assaillirent	ils assailliront

Passé composé: j'ai assailli . . . elle a assailli, *she attacked, she has attacked.*

Participe présent: assaillant, *attacking.*

Conditionnel *I would attack*	**Impératif** *attack*	**Prés. du subj.** *that I attack*	**Imparf. du subj.** *that I attacked*
j' assaillirais		que j' assaille	que j' assaillisse
tu assaillirais	assaille	que tu assailles	que tu assaillisses
il assaillirait		qu'il assaille	qu'il assaillît
nous assaillirions	assaillons	que n. assaillions	que n. assaillissions
vous assailliriez	assaillez	que v. assailliez	que v. assaillissiez
ils assailliraient		qu'ils assaillent	qu'ils assaillissent

Tressaillir, *to start, to jump with surprise,* and **défaillir,** *to faint, to become feeble,* are conjugated like **assaillir.**

**S'ASSEOIR, *to sit down*

Prés. de l'ind. *I sit down*	**Imparfait** *I was sitting down*	**Passé simple** *I sat down*	**Futur simple** *I will sit down*
je m' assieds	je m' asseyais	je m' assis	je m' assiérai
tu t' assieds	tu t' asseyais	tu t' assis	tu t' assiéras
il s' assied	il s' asseyait	il s' assit	il s' assiéra
n.n. asseyons	n.n. asseyions	nous n. assîmes	nous n. assiérons
v.v asseyez	v.v. asseyiez	vous v. assîtes	vous v. assiériez
ils s' asseyent	ils s' asseyaient	ils s' assirent	ils s' assiéront

Passé composé: je me suis assis . . . elle s'est assise, *she sat down.*

Participe présent: s'asseyant, *seating oneself.*

Conditionnel *I would sit down*	**Impératif** *sit down*	**Prés. du subj.** *that I sit down*	**Imparf. du subj.** *that I sat down*
je m' assiérais		que je m' asseye	que je m' assisse
tu t' assiérais	assieds-toi	que tu t' asseyes	que tu t' assisses
ils s' assiérait		qu'il s' asseye	qu'il s' assît
n.n. assiérions	asseyons-nous	que n.n. asseyions	que n.n assissions
v.v. assiériez	asseyez-vous	que v.v. asseyiez	que v.v. assissiez
ils s' assiéraient		qu'ils s' asseyent	qu'ils s' assissent

Rasseoir, *to reseat, to settle,* is conjugated like **asseoir (s'asseoir)**

**AVOIR, *to have*

Prés. de l'ind. *I have*	Imparfait *I used to have*	Passé simple *I had*	Futur simple *I will have*
j' ai tu as il a nous avons vous avez ils ont	j' avais tu avais il avait nous avions vous aviez ils avaient	j' eus tu eus il eut nous eûmes vous eûtes ils eurent	j' aurai tu auras il aura nous aurons vous aurez ils auront
Passé composé: j'ai eu . . . elle a eu, *she had, she has had.* **Participe présent:** ayant, *having.*			
Conditionnel *I would have*	**Impératif** *have*	**Prés. du subj.** *that I have*	**Imparf. du subj.** *that I had*
j' aurais tu aurais il aurait nous aurions vous auriez ils auraient	 aie ayons ayez 	que j' aie que tu aies qu'il ait que n. ayons que v. ayez qu'ils aient	que j' eusse que tu eusses qu'il eût que n. eussions que v. eussiez qu'ils eussent

**BATTRE, *to beat, to defeat*

Prés. de l'ind. *I beat*	Imparfait *I was beating*	Passé simple *I beat*	Futur simple *I will beat*
je bats tu bats il bat nous battons vous battez ils battent	je battais tu battais il battait nous battions vous battiez ils battaient	je battis tu battis il battit nous battîmes vous battîtes ils battirent	je battrai tu battras il battra nous battrons vous battrez ils battront
Passé composé: j'ai battu . . . elle a battu, *she beat, she has beaten.* **Participe présent:** battant, *beating.*			
Conditionnel *I would beat*	**Impératif** *beat*	**Prés. du subj.** *that I beat*	**Imparf. du subj.** *that I beat*
je battrais tu battrais il battrait nous battrions vous battriez ils battraient	 bats battons battez 	que je batte que tu battes qu'il batte que n. battions que v. battiez qu'ils battent	que je battisse que tu battisses qu'il battît que n. battissions que v. battissiez qu'ils battissent

Conjugated like **battre** are: ***abattre,** *to knock down;* ***combattre,** *to combat, to fight (against);* **débattre,** *to debate, to discuss;* **se débattre,** *to struggle;* **s'ébattre,** *to frolic;* **rabattre,** *to lower, to reduce;* **rebattre,** *to beat again.*

**BOIRE, *to drink*

Prés. de l'ind. *I drink*	**Imparfait** *I was drinking*	**Passé simple** *I drank*	**Futur simple** *I will drink*
je bois	je buvais	je bus	je boirai
tu bois	tu buvais	tu bus	tu boiras
il boit	il buvait	il but	il boira
nous buvons	nous buvions	nous bûmes	nous boirons
vous buvez	vous buviez	vous bûtes	vous boirez
ils boivent	ils buvaient	ils burent	ils boiront

Passé composé: j'ai bu . . . elle a bu, *she drank, she has drunk.*

Participe présent: buvant, *drinking.*

Conditionnel *I would drink*	**Impératif** *drink*	**Prés. du subj.** *that I drink*	**Imparf. du subj.** *that I drank*
je boirais		que je boive	que je busse
tu boirais	bois	que tu boives	que tu busses
il boirait		qu'il boive	qu'il bût
nous boirions	buvons	que n. buvions	que n. bussions
vous boiriez	buvez	que v. buviez	que v. bussiez
ils boiraient		qu'ils boivent	qu'ils bussent

---

*BOUILLIR, *to boil*

Prés. de l'ind. *I boil*	**Imparfait** *I was boiling*	**Passé simple** *I boiled*	**Futur simple** *I will boil*
je bous	je bouillais	je bouillis	je bouillirai
tu bous	tu bouillais	tu bouillis	tu bouilliras
il bout	il bouillait	il bouillit	il bouillira
nous bouillons	nous bouillions	nous bouillîmes	nous bouillirons
vous bouillez	vous bouilliez	vous bouillîtes	vous bouillirez
ils bouillent	ils bouillaient	ils bouillirent	ils bouilliront

Passé composé: j'ai bouilli . . . elle à bouilli, *she boiled, she has boiled.*

Participe présent: bouillant, *boiling.*

Conditionnel *I would boil*	**Impératif** *boil*	**Prés. du subj.** *that I boil*	**Imparf. du subj.** *that I boiled*
je bouillirais		que je bouille	que je bouillisse
tu bouillirais	bous	que tu bouilles	que tu bouillisses
ils bouillirait		qu'il bouille	qu'il bouillît
nous bouillirions	bouillons	que n. bouillions	que n. bouillissions
vous bouilliriez	bouillez	que v. bouilliez	que v. bouillissiez
ils bouilliraient		qu'ils bouillent	qu'ils bouillissent

Rebouillir, *to boil again,* is conjugated like **bouillir.**

CLORE, *to close*

Prés. de l'ind. *I close*	Imparfait	Passé simple	Futur simple *I will close*
je clos			je clorai
tu clos			tu cloras
il clôt			il clora
			nous clorons
			vous clorez
ils closent			ils cloront

Passé composé: j'ai clos . . . elle a clos, *she closed, she has closed.*

Participe présent: closant, *closing.*

Conditionnel *I would close*	Impératif *close*	Prés. du subj. *that I close*	Imparf. du subj.
je clorais		que je close	
tu clorait	clos	que tu closes	
il clorait		qu'il close	
nous clorions		que n. closions	
vous cloriez		que v. closiez	
ils cloraient		qu'ils closent	

Enclore, *to enclose, to wall in,* and **éclore,** *to hatch, to blossom,* are conjugated like **clore,** except that we have **il enclot, il éclot** without the ˆ of **il clôt.** The forms **nous enclosons, vous enclosez** exist. **Éclore** is conjugated with **être** in its compound tenses.

---

*CONCLURE, *to conclude, to end*

Prés. de l'ind. *I conclude*	Imparfait *I was concluding*	Passé simple *I concluded*	Futur simple *I will conclude*
je conclus	je concluais	je conclus	je conclurai
tu conclus	tu concluais	tu conclus	tu concluras
il conclut	il concluait	il conclut	il conclura
nous concluons	nous concluions	nous conclûmes	nous conclurons
vous concluez	vous concluiez	vous conclûtes	vous conclurez
ils concluent	ils concluaient	ils conclurent	ils concluront

Passé composé: j'ai conclu . . . elle a conclu, *she concluded, she has concluded.*

Participe présent: concluant, *concluding.*

Conditionnel *I would conclude*	Impératif *conclude*	Prés. du subj. *that I conclude*	Imparf. du subj. *that I concluded*
je conclurais		que je conclue	que je conclusse
tu conclurais	conclus	que tu conclues	que tu conclusses
il conclurait		qu'il conclue	qu'il conclût
nous conclurions	concluons	que n. concluions	que n. conclussions
vous concluriez	concluez	que v. concluiez	que v. conclussiez
ils concluraient		qu'ils concluent	qu'ils conclussent

Exclure, *to exclude,* and **inclure,** *to include,* are conjugated like **conclure,** but the **passé composé** is **j'ai inclus.**

CONFIRE, *to preserve, (fruit, etc.)*

Prés. de l'ind. *I preserve*	**Imparfait** *I was preserving*	**Passé simple** *I preserved*	**Futur simple** *I will preserve*
je confis	je confisais	je confis	je confirai
tu confis	tu confisais	tu confis	tu confiras
il confit	il confisait	il confit	il confira
nous confisons	nous confisions	nous confîmes	nous confirons
vous confisez	vous confisiez	vous confîtes	vous confirez
ils confisent	ils confisaient	ils confirent	ils confiront

Passé composé: j'ai confit . . . elle a confit, *she preserved, she has preserved.*

Participe présent: confisant, *preserving.*

Conditionnel *I would preserve*	**Impératif** *preserve*	**Prés. du subj.** *that I preserve*	**Imparf. du subj.** *that I preserved*
je confirais		que je confise	que je confisse
tu confirais	confis	que tu confises	que tu confisses
il confirait		qu'il confise	qu'il confît
nous confirions	confisons	que n. confisions	que n. confissions
vous confiriez	confisez	que v. confisiez	que v. confissiez
ils confiraient		qu'ils confisent	qu'ils confissent

Conjugated like **confire** are: **déconfire,** *to discomfit;* ***suffire,** *to suffice, to be sufficent;* **circoncire,** *to circumcise;* **frire,** *to fry.*

**CONNAÎTRE, *to know*

Prés. de l'ind. *I know*	**Imparfait** *I used to know*	**Passé simple** *I knew*	**Futur simple** *I will know*
je connais	je connaissais	je connus	je connaîtrai
tu connais	tu connaissais	tu connus	tu connaîtras
il connaît	il connaissait	il connut	il connaîtra
nous connaissons	nous connaissions	nous connûmes	nous connaîtrons
vous connaissez	vous connaissiez	vous connûtes	vous connaîtrez
ils connaissent	ils connaissaient	ils connurent	ils connaîtront

Passé composé: j'ai connu . . . elle a connu, *she knew, she has known.*

Participe présent: connaissant, *knowing.*

Conditionnel *I would know*	**Impératif** *know*	**Prés. du subj.** *that I know*	**Imparf. du subj.** *that I knew*
je connaîtrais		que je connaisse	que je connusse
tu connaîtrais	connais	que tu connaisses	que tu connusses
il connaîtrait		qu'il connaisse	qu'il connût
nous connaîtrions	connaissons	que n. connaissions	que n. connussions
vous connaîtriez	connaissez	que v. connaissiez	que v. connussiez
ils connaîtraient		qu'ils connaissent	qu'ils connussent

Conjugated like **connaître** are: **méconnaître,** *to misappreciate, to disregard;* ***reconnaître,** *to recognise;* ***paraître,** *to appear, to seem;* ***apparaître,** *to appear,* *to become evident;* **comparaître,** *to appear before a court of justice;* ***disparaître,** *to disappear;* **réapparaître,** *to reappear;* **reparaître,** *to reappear;* **transparaître,** *to show through.*

*COUDRE, *to sew, to stitch*

Prés. de l'ind. *I sew*	**Imparfait** *I was sewing*	**Passé simple** *I sewed*	**Futur simple** *I will sew*
je couds	je cousais	je cousis	je coudrai
tu couds	tu cousais	tu cousis	tu coudras
il coud	il cousait	il cousit	il coudra
nous cousons	nous cousions	nous cousîmes	nous coudrons
vous cousez	vous cousiez	vous cousîtes	vous coudrez
ils cousent	ils cousaient	ils cousirent	ils coudront

Passé composé: j'ai cousu . . . elle a cousu, *she sewed, she has sewn.*

Participe présent: cousant, *sewing.*

Conditionnel *I would sew*	**Impératif** *sew*	**Prés. du subj.** *that I sew*	**Imparf. du subj.** *that I sewed*
je coudrais		que je couse	que je cousisse
tu coudrais	couds	que tu couses	que tu cousisses
il coudrait		qu'il couse	qu'il cousît
nous coudrions	cousons	que n. cousions	que n. cousissions
vous coudriez	cousez	que v. cousiez	que v. cousissiez
ils coudraient		qu'ils cousent	qu'ils cousissent

Conjugated like **coudre** are: **découdre,** *to unstitch, to rip up (seam);* **recoudre,** *to sew (garment) up again, to sew (button) on again.*

**COURIR, *to run*

Prés. de l'ind. *I run*	**Imparfait** *I was running*	**Passé simple** *I ran*	**Futur simple** *I will run*
je cours	je courais	je courus	je courrai
tu cours	tu courais	tu courus	tu courras
il court	il courait	il courut	il courra
nous courons	nous courions	nous courûmes	nous courrons
vous courez	vous couriez	vous courûtes	vous courrez
ils courent	ils couraient	ils coururent	ils courront

Passé composé: j'ai couru . . . elle a couru, *she ran, she has ran.*

Participe présent: courant, *running.*

Conditionnel *I would run*	Impératif *run*	Prés. du subj. *that I run*	Imparf. du subj. *that I ran*
je courrais		que je coure	que je courusse
tu courrais	cours	que tu coures	que tu courusse
il courrait		qu'il coure	qu'il courût
nous courrions	courons	que n. courions	que n. courussions
vous courriez	courez	que v. couriez	que v. courussiez
ils courraient		qu'ils courent	qu'ils courussent

Conjugated like **courir** are: ***accourir,** *to hasten (up), to rush up;* **concourir,** *to converge, to unite, to compete;* **discourir,** *to discourse, to air one's opinions;* **encourir,** *to incur (reproaches, expense, etc.);* ***parcourir,** *to travel through, to examine (superficially);* **recourir,** *to run again, to have recourse to s.o., to call in s.o.'s aid;* **secourir,** *to help.* **Accourir** may be conjugated with **être** as well as **avoir: elle a accouru, elle est accourue.**

*CRAINDRE, *to fear, to be afraid (of), to dread*

Prés. de l'ind. *I fear*	Imparfait *I was afraid (of)*	Passé simple *I feared*	Futur simple *I will fear*
je crains	je craignais	je craignis	je craindrai
tu crains	tu craignais	tu craignis	tu craindras
il craint	il craignait	il craignit	il craindra
nous craignons	nous craignions	nous craignîmes	nous craindrons
vous craignez	vous craigniez	vous craignîtes	vous craindrez
ils craignent	ils craignaient	ils craignirent	ils craindront

Passé composé: j'ai craint . . . elle a craint, *she feared, she has been afraid (of)*

Participe présent: craignant, *fearing.*

Conditionnel *I would fear*	Impératif *fear*	Prés. du subj. *that I fear*	Imparf. du subj. *that I feared*
je craindrais		que je craigne	que je craignisse
tu craindrais	crains	que tu craignes	que tu craignisses
il craindrait		qu'il craigne	qu'il craignît
nous craindrions	craignons	que n. craignions	que n. craignissions
vous craindriez	craignez	que v. craigniez	que v. craignissiez
ils craindraient		qu'ils craignent	qu'ils craignissent

Conjugated like **craindre** are: **contraindre,** *to compel, to constrain;* ***plaindre,** *to pity.*

**CROIRE, *to believe*

Prés. de l'ind. *I believe*	Imparfait *I used to believe*	Passé simple *I believed*	Futur simple *I will believe*
je crois	je croyais	je crus	je croirai
tu crois	tu croyais	tu crus	tu croiras
il croit	il croyait	il crut	il croira
nous croyons	nous croyions	nous crûmes	nous croirons
vous croyez	vous croyiez	vous crûtes	vous croirez
ils croient	ils croyaient	ils crurent	ils croiront

Passé composé: j'ai cru . . . elle a cru, *she believed.*

Participe présent: croyant, *believing.*

Conditionnel *I would believe*	**Impératif** *believe*	**Prés. du subj.** *that I believe*	**Imparf. du subj.** *that I believed*
je croirais		que je croie	que je crusse
tu croirais	crois	que tu croies	que tu crusses
il croirait		qu'il croie	qu'il crût
nous croirions	croyons	que n. croyions	que n. crussions
vous croiriez	croyez	que v. croyiez	que v. crussiez
ils croiraient		qu'ils croient	qu'ils crussent

CROÎTRE, *to grow*

Prés. de l'ind. *I grow*	**Imparfait** *I was growing*	**Passé simple** *I grew*	**Futur simple** *I will grow*
je croîs	je croissais	je crûs	je croîtrai
tu croîs	tu croissais	tu crûs	tu croîtras
il croît	il croissait	il crût	il croîtra
nous croissons	nous croissions	nous crûmes	nous croîtrons
vous croissez	vous croissiez	vous crûtes	vous croîtrez
ils croissent	ils croissaient	ils crûrent	ils croîtront

Passé composé: j'ai crû . . . elle a crû, *she grew, she has grown.*

Participe présent: croissant, *growing.*

Conditionnel *I would grow*	**Impératif** *grow*	**Prés. du subj.** *that I grow*	**Imparf. du subj.** *that I grew*
je croîtrais		que je croisse	que je crûsse
tu croîtrais	croîs	que tu croisses	que tu crûsses
il croîtrait		qu'il croisse	qu'il crût
nous croîtrions	croissons	que n. croissions	que n. crûssions
vous croîtriez	croissez	que v. croissiez	que v. crûssiez
ils croîtraient		qu'ils croissent	qu'ils crûssent

Conjugated like **croître** are: **accroître,** *to increase;* **décroître,** *to decrease;* **recroître,** *to grow again.* However, only **croître** has an accent circonflex in **je croîs, tu croîs, je crûs, tu crûs, ils crûrent, que je crûsse . . . crû,** to distinguish these forms from the corresponding ones of the verb **croire.**

*CUEILLIR, *to pick, to gather, to pluck*

Prés. de l'ind. *I pick*	**Imparfait** *I was picking*	**Passé simple** *I picked*	**Futur simple** *I will pick*
je cueille	je cueillais	je cueillis	je cueillerai
tu cueilles	tu cueillais	tu cueillis	tu cueilleras
il cueille	il cueillait	il cueillit	il cueillera
nous cueillons	nous cueillions	nous cueillîmes	nous cueillerons
vous cueillez	vous cueilliez	vous cueillîtes	vous cueillerez
ils cueillent	ils cueillaient	ils cueillirent	ils cueilleront

Passé composé: j'ai cueilli . . . elle a cueilli, *she picked, she has picked.*			
Participe présent: cueillant, *picking.*			
Conditionnel *I would pick* je cueillerais tu cueillerais il cueillerait nous cueillerions vous cueilleriez ils cueilleraient	**Impératif** *pick* cueille cueillons cueillez	**Prés. du subj.** *that I pick* que je cueille que tu cueilles qu'il cueille que n. cueillions que v. cueilliez qu'ils cueillent	**Imparf. du subj.** *that I picked* que je cueillisse que tu cueillisses qu'il cueillît que n. cueillissions que v. cueillissiez qu'ils cueillissent

Conjugated like **cueillir** are: ***accueillir,** *to receive, to greet;* ***recueillir,** *to collect, to gather.*

*CUIRE, *to cook, to bake*

Prés. de l'ind. *I cook*	**Imparfait** *I was cooking*	**Passé simple** *I cooked*	**Futur simple** *I will cook*
je cuis tu cuis il cuit nous cuisons vous cuisez ils cuisent	je cuisais tu cuisais il cuisait nous cuisions vous cuisiez ils cuisaient	je cuisis tu cuisis il cuisit nous cuisîmes vous cuisîtes ils cuisirent	je cuirai tu cuiras il cuira nous cuirons vous cuirez ils cuiront
Passé composé: j'ai cuit . . . elle a cuit, *she cooked, she has cooked.*			
Participe présent: cuisant, *cooking.*			
Conditionnel *I would cook* je cuirais tu cuirais il cuirait nous cuirions vous cuiriez ils cuiraient	**Impératif** *cook* cuis cuisons cuisez	**Prés. du subj.** *that I cook* que je cuise que tu cuises qu'il cuise que n. cuisions que v. cuisiez qu'ils cuisent	**Imparf. du subj.** *that I cooked* que je cuisisse que tu cuisisses qu'il cuisît que n. cuisissions que v. cuisissiez qu'ils cuisissent

Conjugated like **cuire** are: **recuire,** *to cook again, to bake again;* ***conduire,** *to conduct, to drive;* **déduire,** *to deduct, to deduce;* **éconduire,** *to get rid of;* **enduire,** *to plaster, to coat;* **induire,** *to induce, to tempt (s.o. to do sth.);* **introduire,** *to insert, to usher in;* ***produire,** *to produce;* **reconduire,** *to accompany back (to a place), to show out;* ***réduire,** *to reduce;* **reproduire,** *to reproduce;* **séduire,** *to seduce;* **traduire,** *to translate, to prosecute;* ***construire,** *to build, to erect;* **reconstruire,** *to rebuild;* ***détruire,** *to destroy, to demolish;* **instruire,** *to teach, to inform;* **luire,** *to shine;* **reluire,** *to glitter, to gleam;* **nuire,** *to harm;* **s'entre-nuire,** *to harm one another.*

DÉCHOIR *(a), to fall (from high estate, from honour, etc.)*

Prés. de l'ind. *I fall*	**Imparfait**	**Passé simple** *I fell*	**Futur simple** *I will fall*
je déchois tu déchois il déchoit nous déchoyons vous déchoyez ils déchoient		je déchus	je déchoirai tu déchoiras il déchoira nous déchoirons vous déchoirez ils déchoiront also: je décherrai, etc.

Passé composé: *(b)* j'ai déchu . . . elle a déchu, *she fell, she has fallen.*
(c) je suis déchu . . . elle est déchue, *she has fallen*

Participe présent:

Conditionnel *I would fall*	**Impératif**	**Prés. du subj.** *that I fell*	**Imparf. du subj.** *that I fell*
je déchoirais tu déchoirais il déchoirait nous déchoirions vous déchoiriez ils déchoiraient also: je décherrais, etc.		que je déchoie que n. déchoyons	que je déchusse

(a) **Déchoir** is a defective verb, i.e. a verb which is not conjugated in all tenses, moods and persons.
(b) If one emphasizes the falling, **avoir** is the auxiliary.
(c) If one emphasizes the state one is in after the falling, **être** is the auxiliary.

**DEVOIR, *to have to, must, ought, should*

Prés. de l'ind. *I have to*	**Imparfait** *I had to*	**Passé simple** *I had to*	**Futur simple** *I will have to*
je dois tu dois il doit nous devons vous devez ils doivent	je devais tu devais il devait nous devions vous deviez ils devaient	je dus tu dus il dut nous dûmes vous dûtes ils durent	je devrai tu devras il devra nous devrons vous devrez ils devront

Passé composé: j'ai dû . . . elle a dû *(a), she had to.*

Participe présent: devant, *having to.*

Conditionnel *I would have to*	Impératif	Prés. du subj. *that I have to*	Imparf. du subj. *that I had to*
je devrais		que je doive	que je dusse
tu devrais	dois	que tu doives	que tu dusses
il devrait		qu'il doive	qu'il dût
nous devrions	devons	que n. devions	que n. dussions
vous devriez	devez	que v. deviez	que v. dussiez
ils devraient		qu'ils doivent	qu'ils dussent

(a) **due, dus, dues** are without accent circonflex.

Redevoir, *to owe a balance of (a sum on an account, etc.)* is conjugated like **devoir.**

**DIRE, *to say, to tell*

Prés. de l'ind. *I say*	Imparfait *I was saying*	Passé simple *I said*	Futur simple *I will say*
je dis	je disais	je dis	je dirai
tu dis	tu disais	tu dis	tu diras
il dit	il disait	il dit	il dira
nous disons	nous disions	nous dîmes	nous dirons
vous dites	vous disiez	vous dîtes	vous direz
ils disent	ils disaient	ils dirent	ils diront

Passé composé: j'ai dit . . . elle a dit, *she said, she has said.*

Participe présent: disant, *saying.*

Conditionnel *I would say*	Impératif *say, tell*	Prés. du subj. *that I say*	Imparf. du subj. *that I said*
je dirais		que je dise	que je disse
tu dirais	dis	que tu dises	que tu disses
il dirait		qu'il dise	qu'il dît
nous dirions	disons	que n. disions	que n. dissions
vous diriez	dites	que v. disiez	que v. dissiez
ils diraient		qu'ils disent	qu'ils dissent

***Redire,** *to say again, to tell again,* is conjugated like **dire.** The following verbs are also conjugated like **dire** except that, while we have **dites** in the **présent de l'indicatif** and in the **impératif,** we have **contredisez, dédisez, interdisez, médisez** and **prédisez: contredire,** *to contradict, to gainsay;* **dédire,** *to retract a statement, to go back on one's word;* ***interdire,** *to forbid;* **médire,** *to slander, to vilify;* **prédire,** *to predict, to foretell.*

**DORMIR, *to sleep*

Prés. de l'ind. *I sleep*	Imparfait *I was sleeping*	Passé simple *I slept*	Futur simple *I will sleep*
je dors	je dormais	je dormis	je dormirai
tu dors	tu dormais	tu dormis	tu dormiras
il dort	il dormait	il dormit	il dormira
nous dormons	nous dormions	nous dormîmes	nous dormirons
vous dormez	vous dormiez	vous dormîtes	vous dormirez
ils dorment	ils dormaient	ils dormirent	ils dormiront

Passé composé: j'ai dormi . . . elle a dormi, *she slept, she has slept.*

Participe présent: dormant, *sleeping.*

Conditionnel *I would sleep*		**Impératif** *sleep*	**Prés. du subj.** *that I sleep*		**Imparf. du subj.** *that I slept*	
je	dormirais		que je	dorme	que je	dormisse
tu	dormirais	dors	que tu	dormes	que tu	dormisses
il	dormirait		qu'il	dorme	qu'il	dormît
nous	dormirions	dormons	que n.	dormions	que n.	dormissions
vous	dormiriez	dormez	que v.	dormiez	que v.	dormissiez
ils	dormiraient		qu'ils	dorment	qu'ils	dormissent

Conjugated like **dormir** are: **endormir,** *to send (s.o.) to sleep, to benumb (limb, etc.), to hoodwink (s.o.);* **rendormir,** *to send to sleep again.*

**ÉCRIRE, *to write*

Prés. de l'ind. *I write*		**Imparfait** *I was writing*		**Passé simple** *I wrote*		**Futur simple** *I will write*	
j'	écris	j'	écrivais	j'	écrivis	j'	écrirai
tu	écris	tu	écrivais	tu	écrivis	tu	écriras
il	écrit	il	écrivait	il	écrivit	il	écrira
nous	écrivons	nous	écrivions	nous	écrivîmes	nous	écrirons
vous	écrivez	vous	écriviez	vous	écrivîtes	vous	écrirez
ils	écrivent	ils	écrivaient	ils	écrivirent	ils	écriront

Passé composé: j'ai écrit . . . elle a écrit, *she wrote, she has written.*

Participe présent: écrivant, *writing.*

Conditionnel *I would write*		**Impératif** *write*	**Prés. du subj.** *that I write*		**Imparf. du subj.** *that I wrote*	
j'	écrirais		que j'	écrive	que j'	écrivisse
tu	écrirais	écris	que tu	écrives	que tu	écrivisses
il	écrirait		qu'il	écrive	qu'il	écrivît
nous	écririons	écrivons	que n.	écrivions	que n.	écrivissions
vous	écririez	écrivez	que v.	écriviez	que v.	écrivissiez
ils	écriraient		qu'ils	écrivent	qu'ils	écrivissent

Conjugated like **écrire** are: **circonscrire,** *to circumscribe, to encircle;* ***décrire,** *to describe;* ***inscrire,** *to inscribe, to register;* **prescrire,** *to prescribe, to ordain;* **proscrire,** *to proscribe, to outlaw;* **récrire,** *to rewrite;* **réinscrire,** *to inscribe again, to register again;* **souscrire,** *to subscribe, to sign;* **transcrire,** *to transcribe.*

**ENVOYER, *to send*

Prés. de l'ind. *I send*		**Imparfait** *I was sending*		**Passé simple** *I sent*		**Futur simple** *I will send*	
j'	envoie	j'	envoyais	j'	envoyai	j'	enverrai
tu	envoies	tu	envoyais	tu	envoyas	tu	enverras
il	envoie	il	envoyait	il	envoya	il	enverra
nous	envoyons	nous	envoyions	nous	envoyâmes	nous	enverrons
vous	envoyez	vous	envoyiez	vous	envoyâtes	vous	enverrez
ils	envoient	ils	envoyaient	ils	envoyèrent	ils	enverront

Passé composé: j'ai envoyé . . . elle a envoyé, *she sent, she has sent.*

Participe présent: envoyant, *sending.*

Conditionnel *I would send*	**Impératif** *send*	**Prés. du subj.** *that I send*	**Imparf. du subj.** *that I sent*
j' enverrais		que j' envoie	que j' envoyasse
tu enverrais	envoie	que tu envoies	que tu envoyasses
il enverrait		qu'il envoie	qu'il envoyât
nous enverrions	envoyons	que n. envoyions	que n. envoyassions
vous enverriez	envoyez	que v. envoyiez	que v. envoyassiez
ils enverraient		qu'ils envoient	qu'ils envoyassent

***Renvoyer,** *to send back,* is conjugated like **envoyer.**

**ÊTRE, *to be*

Prés. de l'ind. *I am*	**Imparfait** *I used to be*	**Passé simple** *I was*	**Futur simple** *I will be*
je suis	j' étais	je fus	je serai
tu es	tu étais	tu fus	tu seras
il est	il était	il fut	il sera
nous sommes	nous étions	nous fûmes	nous serons
vous êtes	vous étiez	vous fûtes	vous serez
ils sont	ils étaient	ils furent	ils seront

Passé composé: j'ai été . . . elle a été, *she has been, she was.*

Participe présent: étant, *being.*

Conditionnel *I will be*	**Impératif** *be*	**Prés. du subj.** *that I was*	**Imparf. du subj.** *that I will be*
je serais		que je sois	que je fusse
tu serais	sois	que tu sois	que tu fusses
il serait		qu'il soit	qu'il fût
nous serions	soyons	que n. soyons	que n. fussions
vous seriez	soyez	que v. soyez	que v. fussiez
ils seraient		qu'ils soient	qu'ils fussent

FAILLIR, *to fail*

Prés. de l'ind. *I fail*	**Imparfait** *I used to fail*	**Passé simple** *I failed*	**Futur simple** *I will fail*
je faux	je faillais	je faillis	je faillirai
tu faux	tu faillais	tu faillis	tu failliras
il faut	il faillait	il faillit	il faillira
nous faillons	nous faillions	nous faillîmes	nous faillirons
vous faillez	vous failliez	vous faillîtes	vous faillirez
ils faillent	ils faillaient	ils faillirent	ils failliront

Passé composé: j'ai failli . . . elle a failli, *she failed, she has failed.*

Participe présent: faillant, *failing.*

Conditionnel *I would fail*	**Impératif**	**Prés. du subj.** *that I fail*	**Imparf. du subj.** *that I failed*
je faillirais		que je faille	que je faillisse
tu faillirais		que tu failles	que tu faillisses
il faillirait		qu'il faille	qu'il faillît
nous faillirions		que n. faillions	que n. faillissions
vous failliriez		que v. failliez	que v. faillissiez
ils failliraient		qu'ils faillent	qu'ils faillissent

Note the meaning of **faillir** when used with an Infinitive or a noun. **Faillir** + Infinitive (only used in the **passé simple** and in compound tenses), e.g. **il a failli tomber,** *he almost fell.* **Faillir** + noun, e.g. **il a failli à son devoir,** *he failed to do his duty.*

**FAIRE, *to do*

Prés. de l'ind. *I make*	**Imparfait** *I was making*	**Passé simple** *I made*	**Futur simple** *I will make*
je fais	je faisais	je fis	je ferai
tu fais	tu faisais	tu fis	tu feras
il fait	il faisait	il fit	il fera
nous faisons	nous faisions	nous fîmes	nous ferons
vous faites	vous faisiez	vous fîtes	vous ferez
ils font	ils faisaient	ils firent	ils feront

Passé composé: j'ai fait . . . elle a fait, *she made, she has made.*

Participe présent: faisant, *making.*

Conditionnel *I would make*	**Impératif** *make*	**Prés. du subj.** *that I make*	**Imparf. du subj.** *that I made*
je ferais		que je fasse	que je fisse
tu ferais	fais	que tu fasses	que tu fisses
il ferait		qu'il fasse	qu'il fît
nous ferions	faisons	que n. fassions	que n. fissions
vous feriez	faites	que v. fassiez	que v. fissiez
ils feraient		qu'ils fassent	qu'ils fissent

Conjugated like **faire** are: **contrefaire,** *to imitate, to counterfeit;* **défaire,** *to demolish, to undo;* ***refaire,** *to do again, to make again;* ***satisfaire,** *to satisfy;* **surfaire,** *to overcharge, to overrate.*

*FALLOIR, *to be necessary*

Prés. de l'ind. *it is necessary*	**Imparfait** *it was necessary*	**Passé simple** *it was necessary*	**Futur simple** *it will be necessary*
il faut	il fallait	il fallut	il faudra

Passé composé: il a fallu, *it has been necessary, it was necessary.*			
Participe présent: *			
Conditionnel *it would be necessary* il faudrait	**Impératif**	**Prés. du subj.** *that it is necessary* qu'il faille	**Imparf. du subj.** *that it was necessary* qu'il fallût

*FUIR, *to flee, to run away*

Prés. de l'ind. *I flee*	**Imparfait** *I was fleeing*	**Passé simple** *I fled*	**Futur simple** *I will flee*
je fuis	je fuyais	je fuis	je fuirai
tu fuis	tu fuyais	tu fuis	tu fuiras
il fuit	il fuyait	il fuit	il fuira
nous fuyons	nous fuyions	nous fuîmes	nous fuirons
vous fuyez	vous fuyiez	vous fuîtes	vous fuirez
ils fuient	ils fuyaient	ils fuirent	ils fuiront

Passé composé: j'ai fui . . . elle a fui, *she fled, she has fled.*

Participe présent: fuyant, *fleeing.*

Conditionnel *I would flee*	**Impératif** *flee*	**Prés. du subj.** *that I flee*	**Imparf. du subj.** *that I fled*
je fuirais		que je fuie	que je fuisse
tu fuirais	fuis	que tu fuies	que tu fuisses
il fuirait		qu'il fuie	qu'il fuît
nous fuirions	fuyons	que n. fuyions	que n. fuissions
vous fuiriez	fuyez	que v. fuyiez	que v. fuissiez
ils fuiraient		qu'ils fuient	qu'ils fuissent

S'enfuir, *to flee* is conjugated like **fuir,** but, like all reflexive verbs the compound tenses are conjugated with **être: je me suis enfui, . . . elle s'est enfuie.**

GÉSIR, *to lie (helpless or dead)*

Prés. de l'ind. *I lie*	**Imparfait** *I was lying*
je gis	je gisais
tu gis	tu gisais
il git	il gisait
nous gisons	nous gisions
vous gisez	vous gisiez
ils gisent	ils gisaient

Participe présent: gisant, *lying.*

HAÏR, *to hate, to detest*

Prés. de l'ind. *I hate*	Imparfait *I used to hate*	Passé simple *I hated*	Futur simple *I will hate*
je hais	je haïssais	je haïs	je haïrai
tu hais	tu haïssais	tu haïs	tu haïras
il hait	il haïssait	il haït	il haïra
nous haïssons	nous haïssions	nous haïmes	nous haïrons
vous haïssez	vous haïssiez	vous haïtes	vous haïrez
ils haïssent	ils haïssaient	ils haïrent	ils haïront

Passé composé: j'ai haï . . . elle a haï, *she hated, she has hated.*

Participe présent: haïssant, *hating.*

Conditionnel *I would hate*	Impératif *hate*	Prés. du subj. *that I hate*	Imparf. du subj. *that I hated*
je haïrais		que je haïsse	que je haïsse
tu haïrais	hais	que tu haïsses	que tu haïsses
il haïrait		qu'il haïsse	qu'il haït
nous haïrions	haïssons	que n. haïssions	que n. haïssions
vous haïriez	haïssez	que v. haïssiez	que v. haïssiez
ils haïraient		qu'ils haïssent	qu'ils haïssent

JOINDRE, *to join*

Prés. de l'ind. *I join*	Imparfait *I was joining*	Passé simple *I joined*	Futur simple *I will join*
je joins	je joignais	je joignis	je joindrai
tu joins	tu joignais	tu joignis	tu joindras
il joint	il joignait	il joignit	il joindra
nous joignons	nous joignions	nous joignîmes	nous joindrons
vous joignez	vous joigniez	vous joignîtes	vous joindrez
ils joignent	ils joignaient	ils joignirent	ils joindront

Passé composé: j'ai joint . . . elle a joint, *she joined, she has joined.*

Participe présent: joignant, *joining.*

Conditionnel *I would join*	Impératif *join*	Prés. du subj. *that I join*	Imparf. du subj. *that I joined*
je joindrais		que je joigne	que je joignisse
tu joindrais	joins	que tu joignes	que tu joignisses
il joindrait		qu'il joigne	qu'il joignît
nous joindrions	joignons	que n. joignions	que n. joignissions
vous joindriez	joignez	que v. joigniez	que v. joignissiez
ils joindraient		qu'ils joignent	qu'ils joignissent

Conjugated like **joindre** are: **adjoindre,** *to unite, to associate (with);* **conjoindre,** *to join in marriage;* **disjoindre,** *to disjoin, to sever;* **enjoindre, enjoindre à quelqu'un de faire quelque chose,** *to call upon s.o. to do sth.,* ***rejoindre,** *to* *rejoin, to catch up (again).* The archaic verbs **oindre,** *to anoint (kings, etc.);* and **poindre,** *to dawn, to sprout,* are also conjugated like **joindre,** but are very seldom used and not in all tenses.

**LIRE, *to read*

Prés. de l'ind. *I read*	**Imparfait** *I was reading*	**Passé simple** *I read*	**Futur simple** *I will read*
je lis	je lisais	je lus	je lirai
tu lis	tu lisais	tu lus	tu liras
il lit	il lisait	il lut	il lira
nous lisons	nous lisions	nous lûmes	nous lirons
vous lisez	vous lisiez	vous lûtes	vous lirez
ils lisent	ils lisaient	ils lurent	ils liront

Passé composé: j'ai lu . . . elle a lu, *she read, she has read.*

Participe présent: lisant, *reading.*

Conditionnel *I would read*	**Impératif** *read*	**Prés. du subj.** *that I read*	**Imparf. du subj.** *that I read*
je lirais		que je lise	que je lusse
tu lirais	lis	que tu lises	que tu lusses
il lirait		qu'il lise	qu'il lût
nous lirions	lisons	que n. lisions	que n. lussions
vous liriez	lisez	que v. lisiez	que v. lussiez
ils liraient		qu'ils lisent	qu'ils lussent

Conjugated like **lire** are: ***élire,** *to elect, to choose;* **réélire,** *to re-elect;* **relire,** *to read (over) again.*

**METTRE, *to put, to place*

Prés. de l'ind. *I put*	**Imparfait** *I was putting*	**Passé simple** *I put*	**Futur simple** *I will put*
je mets	je mettais	je mis	je mettrai
tu mets	tu mettais	tu mis	tu mettras
il met	il mettait	il mit	il mettra
nous mettons	nous mettions	nous mîmes	nous mettrons
vous mettez	vous mettiez	vous mîtes	vous mettrez
ils mettent	ils mettaient	ils mirent	ils mettront

Passé composé: j'ai mis . . . elle a mis, *she put, she has put.*

Participe présent: mettant, *putting.*

Conditionnel *I would put*	Impératif *put*	Prés. du subj. *that I put*	Imparf. du subj. *that I put*
je mettrais		que je mette	que je misse
tu mettrais	mets	que tu mettes	que tu misses
il mettrait		qu'il mette	qu'il mît
nous mettrions	mettons	que n. mettions	que n. missions
vous mettriez	mettez	que v. mettiez	que v. missiez
ils mettraient		qu'ils mettent	qu'ils missent

Conjugated like **mettre** are: ***admettre,** *to admit, to allow;* **commettre,** *to commit;* **compromettre,** *to compromise (s.o.), to accept arbitration;* **démettre,** *to dislocate (joint);* **émettre,** *to emit, to broadcast, to issue;* **s'entremettre** (conjugated with **être**), *to intervene, to act as a go-between;* **omettre,** *to omit, to leave out;* ***permettre,** *to permit, to allow;* ***promettre,** *to promise;* ***remettre,** *to put back (again), to postpone;* ***soumettre,** *to subdue;* ***se soumettre** (conjugated with **être**), *to submit, to yield;* **transmettre,** *to transmit, to transfer.*

MOUDRE, *to grind (coffee)*

Prés. de l'ind. *I grind*	Imparfait *I was grinding*	Passé simple *I ground*	Futur simple *I will grind*
je mouds	je moulais	je moulus	je moudrai
tu mouds	tu moulais	tu moulus	tu moudras
il moud	il moulait	il moulut	il moudra
nous moulons	nous moulions	nous moulûmes	nous moudrons
vous moulez	vous mouliez	vous moulûtes	vous moudrez
ils moulent	ils moulaient	ils moulurent	ils moudront

Passé composé: j'ai moulu . . . elle a moulu, *she ground, she had ground.*

Participe présent: moulant, *grinding.*

Conditionnel *I would grind*	Impératif *grind*	Prés. du subj. *that I grind*	Imparf. du subj. *that I ground*
je moudrais		que je moule	que je moulusse
tu moudrais	mouds	que tu moules	que tu moulusses
il moudrait		qu'il moule	qu'il moulût
nous moudrions	moulons	que n. moulions	que n. moulussions
vous moudriez	moulez	que v. mouliez	que v. moulussiez
ils moudraient		qu'ils moulent	qu'ils moulussent

Conjugated like **moudre** are: **émoudre,** *to grind, to sharpen;* **rémoudre,** *to re-sharpen, to regrind (tool);* **remoudre,** *to regrind (corn, coffee).*

*MOURIR, *to die*

Prés. de l'ind. *I die*	Imparfait *I was dying*	Passé simple *I died*	Futur simple *I will die*
je meurs	je mourais	je mourus	je mourrai
tu meurs	tu mourais	tu mourus	tu mourras
il meurt	il mourait	il mourut	il mourra
nous mourons	nous mourions	nous mourûmes	nous mourrons
vous mourez	vous mouriez	vous mourûtes	vous mourrez
ils meurent	ils mouraient	ils moururent	ils mourront

Passé composé: je suis mort . . . elle est morte, *she died, she is dead, she has died.*			
Participe présent: mourant, *dying.*			

Conditionnel *I would die*	**Impératif** *die*	**Prés. du subj.** *that I die*	**Imparf. du subj.** *that I died*
je mourrais		que je meure	que je mourusse
tu mourrais	meurs	que tu meures	que tu mourusses
il mourrait		qu'il meure	qu'il mourût
nous mourrions	mourons	que n. mourions	que n. mourussions
vous mourriez	mourez	que v. mouriez	que v. mourussiez
ils mourraient		qu'ils meurent	qu'ils mourussent

MOUVOIR, *to move*

Prés. de l'ind. *I move*	**Imparfait** *I was moving*	**Passé simple** *I moved*	**Futur simple** *I will move*
je meus	je mouvais	je mus	je mouvrai
tu meus	tu mouvais	tu mus	tu mouvras
il meut	il mouvait	il mut	il mouvra
nous mouvons	nous mouvions	nous mûmes	nous mouvrons
vous mouvez	vous mouviez	vous mûtes	vous mouvrez
ils meuvent	ils mouvaient	ils murent	ils mouvront

Passé composé: j'ai mû . . . elle a mû, *she moved, she has moved.*

Participe présent: mouvant, *moving.*

Conditionnel *I would move*	**Impératif** *move*	**Prés. du subj.** *that I move*	**Imparf. du subj.** *that I moved*
je mouvrais		que je meuve	que je musse
tu mouvrais	meus	que tu meuves	que tu musses
il mouvrait		qu'il meuve	qu'il mût
nous mouvrions	mouvons	que n. mouvions	que n. mussions
vous mouvriez	mouvez	que v. mouviez	que v. mussiez
ils mouvraient		qu'ils meuvent	qu'ils mussent

***Emouvoir,** *to stir up, to rouse, to affect,* and **promouvoir,** *to promote,* are conjugated like **mouvoir,** but have no circumflex accent in the past participle: **ému, promu.**

*NAÎTRE, *to be born*

Prés. de l'ind. *I am born*	**Imparfait** *I was being born*	**Passé simple** *I was born*	**Futur simple** *I will be born*
je nais	je naissais	je naquis	je naîtrai
tu nais	tu naissais	tu naquis	tu naîtras
il naît	il naissait	il naquit	il naîtra
nous naissons	nous naissions	nous naquîmes	nous naîtrons
vous naissez	vous naissiez	vous naquîtes	vous naîtrez
ils naissent	ils naissaient	ils naquirent	ils naîtront

Passé composé: je suis né . . . elle est née, *she is born.*
Participe présent: naissant, *being born.*

Conditionnel *I would be born*	**Impératif** *be born*	**Prés. du subj.** *that I am born*	**Imparf. du subj.** *that I was born*
je naîtrais		que je naisse	que je naquisse
tu naîtrais	nais	que tu naisses	que tu naquisses
il naîtrait		qu'il naisse	qu'il naquît
nous naîtrions	naissons	que n. naissions	que n. naquissions
vous naîtriez	naissez	que v. naissiez	que v. naquissiez
ils naîtraient		qu'ils naissent	qu'ils naquissent

Renaître, *to be born again,* is conjugated like **naître.**

OUÏR, *to hear*

Prés. de l'ind. *I hear*	**Imparfait** *I was hearing*	**Passé simple** *I heard*	**Futur simple** *I will hear*
j' ois	j' oyais	j' ouïs	j' ouïrai
tu ois	tu oyais	tu ouïs	tu ouïras
il oit	il oyait	il ouït	il ouïra
nous oyons	nous oyions	nous ouîmes	nous ouïrons
vous oyez	vous oyiez	vous ouîtes	vous ouïrez
ils oient	ils oyaient	ils ouïrent	ils ouïront

Passé composé: j'ai ouï . . . elle a ouï, *she heard, she has heard.*

Participe présent: oyant, *hearing.*

Conditionnel *I would hear*	**Impératif** *hear*	**Prés. du subj.** *that I hear*	**Imparf. du subj.** *that I heard*
j' ouïrais		que j' oie	que j' ouisse
tu ouïrais	ois	que tu oies	que tu ouisses
il ouïrait		qu'il oie	qu'il ouît
nous ouïrions	oyons	que n. oyions	que n. ouissions
vous ouïriez	oyez	que v. oyiez	que v. ouissiez
ils ouïraient		qu'ils oient	qu'ils ouissent

Ouïr is an obsolete verb. Its place is now taken by **entendre.**

**OUVRIR, *to open*

Prés. de l'ind. *I open*	**Imparfait** *I am opening*	**Passé simple** *I opened*	**Futur simple** *I will open*
j' ouvre	j' ouvrais	j' ouvris	j' ouvrirai
tu ouvres	tu ouvrais	tu ouvris	tu ouvriras
il ouvre	il ouvrait	il ouvrit	il ouvrira
nous ouvrons	nous ouvrions	nous ouvrîmes	nous ouvrirons
vous ouvrez	vous ouvriez	vous ouvrîtes	vous ouvrirez
ils ouvrent	ils ouvraient	ils ouvrirent	ils ouvriront

Passé composé: j'ai ouvert . . . elle a ouvert, *she opened, she has opened.*

Participe présent: ouvrant, *opening.*

Conditionnel *I would open*	**Impératif** *open*	**Prés. du subj.** *that I open*	**Imparf. du subj.** *that I opened*
j' ouvrirais		que j' ouvre	que j' ouvrisse
tu ouvrirais	ouvre	que tu ouvres	que tu ouvrisses
il ouvrirait		qu'il ouvre	qu'il ouvrît
nous ouvririons	ouvrons	que n. ouvrions	que n. ouvrissions
vous ouvririez	ouvrez	que v. ouvriez	que v. ouvrissiez
ils ouvriraient		qu'ils ouvrent	qu'ils ouvrissent

Conjugated like **ouvrir** are: **rouvrir,** *to re-open;* ***couvrir,** *to cover;* **recouvrir,** *to re-cover;* ***offrir,** *to offer;* ***souffrir,** *to suffer,* and their compounds, e.g. ***découvrir,** *to discover;* **recouvrir,** *to re-cover (roof, etc.), to hide, to mask;* **entrouvrir,** *to half-open, to set (door) ajar.*

PAÎTRE, *to graze, to feed*

Prés. de l'ind. *I graze*	**Imparfait** *I was grazing*	**Passé simple**	**Futur simple** *I will graze*
je pais	je paissais		je paîtrai
tu pais	tu paissais		tu paîtras
il paît	il paissait		il paîtra
nous paissons	nous paissions		nous paîtrons
vous paissez	vous paissiez		vous paîtrez
ils paissent	ils paissaient		ils paîtront

Passé composé:

Participe présent:

Conditionnel *I would graze*	**Impératif** *graze*	**Prés. du subj.** *that I graze*	**Imparf. du subj.**
je paîtrais		que je paisse	
tu paîtrais	pais	que tu paisses	
il paîtrait		qu'il paisse	
nous paîtrions		que n. paissions	
vous paîtriez	paissez	que v. paissiez	
ils paîtraient		qu'ils paissent	

Repaître, *to graze, to feed,* is conjugated like **paître** but is also conjugated in the

Passé simple *I grazed*	**Passé composé** *(a)* *I have grazed*		**Imparf. du subj.** *that I grazed*
je repus	j'ai repu		que je repusse

(a) as well as in all the other compound tenses.

*PEINDRE, *to paint*

Prés. de l'ind.	Imparfait	Passé simple	Futur simple
I paint	*I was painting*	*I painted*	*I will paint*
je peins	je peignais	je peignis	je peindrai
tu peins	tu peignais	tu peignis	tu peindras
il peint	il peignait	il peignit	il peindra
nous peignons	nous peignions	nous peignîmes	nous peindrons
vous peignez	vous peigniez	vous peignîtes	vous peindrez
ils peignent	ils peignaient	ils peignirent	ils peindront

Passé composé: j'ai peint . . . elle a peint, *she painted, she has painted.*

Participe présent: peignant, *painting.*

Conditionnel	Impératif	Prés. du subj.	Imparf. du subj.
I would paint	*paint*	*that I paint*	*that I painted*
je peindrais		que je peigne	que je peignisse
tu peindrais	peins	que tu peignes	que tu peignisses
il peindrait		qu'il peigne	qu'il peignît
nous peindrions	peignons	que n. peignions	que n. peignissions
vous peindriez	peignez	que v. peigniez	que v. peignissiez
ils peindraient		qu'ils peignent	qu'ils peignissent

Conjugated like **peindre** are: **astreindre,** *to compel;* **atteindre,** *to reach;* **ceindre,** *to gird on, to buckle on, to encircle;* **déteindre,** *to fade;* **empreindre,** *to imprint;* **enceindre,** *to gird, to surround;* **enfreindre,** *to infringe;* **éteindre,** *to extinquish, to put (light) out;* **feindre,** *to feing, to simulate, to sham;* **geindre,** *to whine, to whimper;* **restreindre,** *to restrict, to curtail;* **teindre,** *to dye, to colour.*

*PLAIRE, *to please*

Prés. de l'ind.	Imparfait	Passé simple	Futur simple
I please	*I was pleasing*	*I was pleased*	*I will please*
je plais	je plaisais	je plus	je plairai
tu plais	tu plaisais	tu plus	tu plairas
il plaît	il plaisait	il plut	il plaira
nous plaisons	nous plaisions	nous plûmes	nous plairons
vous plaisez	vous plaisiez	vous plûtes	vous plairez
ils plaisent	ils plaisaient	ils plurent	ils plairont

Passé composé: j'ai plu . . . elle a plu, *she pleased, she has pleased.*

Participe présent: plaisant, *pleasing.*

Conditionnel	Impératif	Prés. du subj.	Imparf. du subj.
I would please	*please*	*that I please*	*that I was pleased*
je plairais		que je plaise	que je plusse
tu plairais	plais	que tu plaises	que tu plusses
il plairait		qu'il plaise	qu'il plût
nous plairions	plaisons	que n. plaisions	que n. plussions
vous plairiez	plaisez	que v. plaisiez	que v. plussiez
ils plairaient		qu'ils plaisent	qu'ils plussent

Conjugated like **plaire** are: **complaire,** *to humour;* **déplaire,** *to displease;* ***se taire** *(conjugated with* **être**), *to be or remain silent.* However, **taire** has no circumflex accent in the **présent de l'indicatif:** il se tait.

**PLEUVOIR, *to rain*

Prés. de l'ind. *It rains* il pleut	**Imparfait** *It was raining* il pleuvait	**Passé simple** *It rained* il plut	**Futur simple** *It will rain* il pleuvra
Passé composé: il a plu, *it rained, it has been raining.* **Participe présent:** pleuvant, *raining.*			
Conditionnel *It would rain* il pleuvrait	**Impératif**	**Prés. du subj.** *that it rains* qu'il pleuve	**Imparf. du subj.** *that it rained* qu'il plût

Though **pleuvoir** is an impersonal verb (i.e. only used with "it"), one must note such expressions as: **les coups pleuvent,** *the blows come fast,* **les coups pleuvaient.**

POURVOIR, *to provide*

Prés. de l'ind. *I provide*		**Imparfait** *I was providing*		**Passé simple** *I provided*		**Futur simple** *I will provide*	
je	pourvois	je	pourvoyais	je	pourvus	je	pourvoirai
tu	pourvois	tu	pourvoyais	tu	pourvus	tu	pourvoiras
il	pourvoit	il	pourvoyait	il	pourvut	il	pourvoira
nous	pourvoyons	nous	pourvoyions	nous	pourvûmes	nous	pourvoirons
vous	pourvoyez	vous	pourvoyiez	vous	pourvûtes	vous	pourvoirez
ils	pourvoient	ils	pourvoyaient	ils	pourvurent	ils	pourvoiront

Passé composé: j'ai pourvu . . . elle a pourvu, *she provided, she has provided.*

Participe présent: pourvoyant, *providing.*

Conditionnel *I would provide*		**Impératif** *provide*	**Prés. du subj.** *that I provide*		**Imparf. du subj.** *that I provided*	
je	pourvoirais		que je	pourvoie	que je	pourvusse
tu	pourvoirais	pourvois	que tu	pourvoies	que tu	pourvusses
il	pourvoirait		qu'il	pourvoie	qu'il	pourvût
nous	pourvoirions	pourvoyons	que n.	pourvoyions	que n.	pourvussions
vous	pourvoiriez	pourvoyez	que v.	pourvoyiez	que v.	pourvussiez
ils	pourvoiraient		qu'ils	pourvoient	qu'ils	pourvussent

Dépourvoir, *to deprive,* is conjugated like **pourvoir** but is only used in the Infinitive, the Past Participle, and the compound tenses.

**POUVOIR, *to be able, "can", to be allowed*

Prés. de l'ind. *I can*	**Imparfait** *I was able to*	**Passé simple** *I could*	**Futur simple** *I will be able to*
je peux*(a)*	je pouvais	je pus	je pourrai
tu peux	tu pouvais	tu pus	tu pourras
il peut	il pouvait	il put	il pourra
nous pouvons	nous pouvions	nous pûmes	nous pourrons
vous pouvez	vous pouviez	vous pûtes	vous pourrez
ils peuvent	ils pouvaient	ils purent	ils pourront
(a) or je puis			

Passé composé: j'ai pu . . . elle a pu, *she could, she has been able to.*

Participe présent: pouvant, *being able.*

Conditionnel *I would be able*	**Impératif**	**Prés. du subj.** *that I can*	**Imparf. du subj.** *that I could*
je pourrais		que je puisse	que je pusse
tu pourrais		que tu puisses	que tu pusses
il pourrait		qu'il puisse	qu'il pût
nous pourrions		que n. puissions	que n. pussions
vous pourriez		que v. puissiez	que v. pussiez
ils pourraient		qu'ils puissent	qu'ils pussent

N.B. **Puis-je** is used, not **peux-je. Il se peut que** means "it is possible that" and is followed by the Subjunctive.

** PRENDRE, *to take*

Prés. de l'ind. *I take*	**Imparfait** *I was taking*	**Passé simple** *I took*	**Futur simple** *I will take*
je prends	je prenais	je pris	je prendrai
tu prends	tu prenais	tu pris	tu prendras
il prend	il prenait	il prit	il prendra
nous prenons	nous prenions	nous prîmes	nous prendrons
vous prenez	vous preniez	vous prîtes	vous prendrez
ils prennent	ils prenaient	ils prirent	ils prendront

Passé composé: j'ai pris . . . elle a pris, *she took, she has taken.*

Participe présent: prenant, *taking.*

Conditionnel *I would take*	**Impératif** *take*	**Prés. du subj.** *that I take*	**Imparf. du subj.** *that I took*
je prendrais		que je prenne	que je prisse
tu prendrais	prends	que tu prennes	que tu prisses
il prendrait		qu'il prenne	qu'il prît
nous prendrions	prenons	que n. prenions	que n. prissions
vous prendriez	prenez	que v. preniez	que v. prissiez
ils prendraient		qu'ils prennent	qu'ils prissent

Conjugated like **prendre** are: ***apprendre,** *to learn;* ***comprendre,** *to understand;* ***entreprendre,** *to undertake;* **s'éprendre de** (conjugated with **être**), *to fall in love with;* ***reprendre,** *to take back, to take again;* **se reprendre** (with **être**), *to correct oneself (in speaking);* ***surprendre,** *to surprise.*

**RECEVOIR, *to receive*

Prés. de l'ind. *I receive*	Imparfait *I was receiving*	Passé simple *I received*	Futur simple *I will receive*
je reçois	je recevais	je reçus	je recevrai
tu reçois	tu recevais	tu reçus	tu recevras
il reçoit	il recevait	il reçut	il recevra
nous recevons	nous recevions	nous reçûmes	nous recevrons
vous recevez	vous receviez	vous reçûtes	vous recevrez
ils reçoivent	ils recevaient	ils reçurent	ils recevront

Passé composé: j'ai reçu . . . elle a reçu, *she received, she has received*

Participe présent: recevant, *receiving*

Conditionnel *I would receive*	Impératif *receive*	Prés. du subj. *that I receive*	Imparf. du subj. *that I received*
je recevrais		que je reçoive	que je reçusse
tu recevrais	reçois	que tu reçoives	que tu reçusses
il recevrait		qu'il reçoive	qu'il reçût
nous recevrions	recevons	que n. recevions	que n. reçussions
vous recevriez	recevez	que v. receviez	que v. reçussiez
ils recevraient		qu'ils reçoivent	qu'ils reçussent

Conjugated like **recevoir** are: ***apercevoir,** *to perceive, to see;* **concevoir,** *to conceive;* **décevoir,** *to deceive, to disappoint;* **percevoir,** *to perceive, to discern, to collect (taxes).*

---

*RÉSOUDRE, *to resolve, to clear up*

Prés. de l'ind. *I resolve*	Imparfait *I was resolving*	Passé simple *I resolved*	Futur simple *I will resolve*
je résous	je résolvais	je résolus	je résoudrai
tu résous	tu résolvais	tu résolus	tu résoudras
il résout	il résolvait	il résolut	il résoudra
nous résolvons	nous résolvions	nous résolûmes	nous résoudrons
vous résolvez	vous résolviez	vous résolûtes	vous résoudrez
ils résolvent	ils résolvaient	ils résolurent	ils résoudront

Passé composé: j'ai résolu . . . elle a résolu, *she resolved, she has resolved.*

Participe présent: résolvant, *resolving.*

Conditionnel *I would resolve*	Impératif *resolve*	Prés. du subj. *that I resolve*	Imparf. du subj. *that I resolved*
je résoudrais		que je résolve	que je résolusse
tu résoudrais	résous	que tu résolves	que tu résolusses
il résoudrait		qu'il résolve	qu'il résolût
nous résoudrions	résolvons	que n. résolvions	que n. résolussions
vous résoudriez	résolvez	que v. résolviez	que v. résolussiez
ils résoudraient		qu'ils résolvent	qu'ils résolussent

Conjugated like **résoudre** are: **absoudre,** *to forgive, to absolve,* and **dissoudre,** *to dissolve, to melt.*

Absoudre and **dissoudre** are not conjugated in the **passé composé,** the **impératif,** or the **imparfait du subjonctif.** Their past participle is **absous** m., **absoute** f., **dissous** m., **dissoute** f.

**RIRE, *to laugh*

Prés. de l'ind. *I laugh*	**Imparfait** *I was laughing*	**Passé simple** *I laughed*	**Futur simple** *I will laugh*
je ris	je riais	je ris	je rirai
tu ris	tu riais	tu ris	tu riras
il rit	il riait	il rit	il rira
nous rions	nous riions	nous rîmes	nous rirons
vous riez	vous riiez	vous rîtes	vous rirez
ils rient	ils riaient	ils rirent	ils riront

Passé composé: j'ai ri . . . elle a ri, *she laughed, she has laughed.*

Participe présent: riant, *laughing.*

Conditionnel *I would laugh*	**Impératif** *laugh*	**Prés. du subj.** *that I laugh*	**Imparf. du subj.** *that I laughed*
je rirais		que je rie	que je risse
tu rirais	ris	que tu ries	que tu risses
il rirait		qu'il rie	qu'il rît
nous ririons	rions	que n. riions	que n. rissions
vous ririez	riez	que v. riiez	que v. rissiez
ils riraient		qu'ils rient	qu'ils rissent

Sourire, *to smile,* is conjugated like **rire.**

ROMPRE, *to break*

Rompre, as well as **corrompre,** *to corrupt,* and ***interrompre,** *to interrupt,* are conjugated like **vendre** except for the fact that in the 3rd person singular of the Present Indicative they add a **t** to the stem **romp: il rompt,** whereas we have **il vend.**

**SAVOIR, *to know*

Prés. de l'ind. *I know*	**Imparfait** *I used to know*	**Passé simple** *I knew*	**Futur simple** *I will know*
je sais	je savais	je sus	je saurai
tu sais	tu savais	tu sus	tu sauras
il sait	il savait	il sut	il saura
nous savons	nous savions	nous sûmes	nous saurons
vous savez	vous saviez	vous sûtes	vous saurez
ils savent	ils savaient	ils surent	ils sauront

Passé composé: j'ai su . . . elle a su, *she knew, she has known.*

Participe présent: sachant, knowing.

Conditionnel *I would know*	Impératif *know*	Prés. du subj. *that I know*	Imparf. du subj. *that I knew*
je saurais		que je sache	que je susse
tu saurais	sache	que tu saches	que tu susses
il saurait		qu'il sache	qu'il sût
nous saurions	sachons	que n. sachions	que n. sussions
vous sauriez	sachez	que v. sachiez	que v. sussiez
ils sauraient		qu'ils sachent	qu'ils sussent

**SENTIR, *to feel, to smell of (sth.)*

Prés. de l'ind. *I feel*	Imparfait *I was feeling*	Passé simple *I felt*	Futur simple *I will feel*
je sens	je sentais	je sentis	je sentirai
tu sens	tu sentais	tu sentis	tu sentiras
il sent	il sentait	il sentit	il sentira
nous sentons	nous sentions	nous sentîmes	nous sentirons
vous sentez	vous sentiez	vous sentîtes	vous sentirez
ils sentent	ils sentaient	ils sentirent	ils sentiront

Passé composé: j'ai senti . . . elle a senti, *she felt, she has felt.*

Participe présent: sentant, *feeling.*

Conditionnel *I would feel*	Impératif *feel*	Prés. du subj. *that I feel*	Imparf. du subj. *that I felt*
je sentirais		que je sente	que je sentisse
tu sentirais	sens	que tu sentes	que tu sentisses
il sentirait		qu'il sente	qu'il sentît
nous sentirions	sentons	que n. sentions	que n. sentissions
vous sentiriez	sentez	que v. sentiez	que v. sentissiez
ils sentiraient		qu'ils sentent	qu'ils sentissent

Conjugated like **sentir** are: **consentir,** *to consent, to agree;* **pressentir,** *to have a foreboding;* **ressentir,** *to feel, to experience;* ***mentir,** *to lie, to tell lies;* **démentir,** *to contradict, to deny;* ***partir,** *to part, to depart, to set out;* **départir,** *to divide, to deal out;* ***repartir,** *to set out again;* **se repentir,** *to repent, to be sorry for sth.;* ***sortir,** *to go or come out, to leave the room or the house;* **ressortir,** *to go or come out again.* **Partir, repartir, se repentir, sortir** and **ressortir** are conjugated with **être** in their compound tenses; see also p. 5, no. 3.

SEOIR (1), *to suit, to become*

Prés. de l'ind. *it suits*	Imparfait *it used to suit*	Passé simple	Futur simple *it will suit*
il sied	il seyait		il siéra
ils siéent	ils seyaient		ils siéront

Participe présent: séant (seyant), *suiting*			
Conditionnel *it would suit* il siérait ils siéraient	**Impératif**	**Prés. du subj.** *that it suits* qu'il siée qu'ils siéent	**Imparf. du subj.**

(1) Seoir is a defective verb.

** SERVIR, *to serve, to be useful (to)*

Prés. de l'ind. *I serve*	**Imparfait** *I was serving*	**Passé simple** *I served*	**Futur simple** *I will serve*
je sers	je servais	je servis	je servirai
tu sers	tu servais	tu servis	tu serviras
il sert	il servait	il servit	il servira
nous servons	nous servions	nous servîmes	nous servirons
vous servez	vous serviez	vous servîtes	vous servirez
ils servent	ils servaient	ils servirent	ils serviront

Passé composé: j'ai servi . . . elle a servi, *she served, she has served.*

Participe présent: servant, *serving.*

Conditionnel *I would serve*	**Impératif** *serve*	**Prés. du subj.** *that I serve*	**Imparf. du subj.** *that I served*
je servirais		que je serve	que je servisse
tu servirais	sers	que tu serves	que tu servisses
il servirait		qu'il serve	qu'il servît
nous servirions	servons	que n. servions	que n. servissions
vous serviriez	servez	que v. serviez	que v. servissiez
ils serviraient		qu'ils servent	qu'ils servissent

Conjugated like **servir** are: **desservir,** *to clear the table, to do a disservice;* **resservir,** *to serve again, to be used again.* Note that **asservir,** *to enslave,* is conjugated like **finir,** p. 12.

** SUIVRE, *to follow*

Prés. de l'ind. *I follow*	**Imparfait** *I was following*	**Passé simple** *I followed*	**Futur simple** *I will follow*
je suis	je suivais	je suivis	je suivrai
tu suis	tu suivais	tu suivis	tu suivras
il suit	il suivait	il suivit	il suivra
nous suivons	nous suivions	nous suivîmes	nous suivrons
vous suivez	vous suiviez	vous suivîtes	vous suivrez
ils suivent	ils suivaient	ils suivirent	ils suivront

Passé composé: j'ai suivi . . . elle a suivi, *she followed , she has followed.*

Participe présent: suivant, *following.*

Conditionnel *I would follow*	**Impératif** *follow*	**Prés. du subj.** *that I follow*	**Imparf. du subj.** *that I followed*
je suivrais		que je suive	que je suivisse
tu suivrais	suis	que tu suives	que tu suivisses
il suivrait		qu'il suive	qu'il suivît
nous suivrions	suivons	que n. suivions	que n. suivissions
vous suivriez	suivez	que v. suiviez	que v. suivissiez
ils suivraient		qu'ils suivent	qu'ils suivissent

Conjugated like **suivre** are: ***poursuivre,** *to pursue;* **s'ensuivre** (with **être**), *to follow, to ensue, to result,* but it is used only in the third person. **Il s'ensuit que je n'ai plus le sou,** *the result is that I have not a penny left.*

SURSEOIR, *to delay a judgement, to stay proceedings*

Prés. de l'ind. *I delay*	**Imparfait** *I was delaying*	**Passé simple** *I delayed*	**Futur simple** *I will delay*
je sursois	je sursoyais	je sursis	je surseoirai
tu sursois	tu sursoyais	tu sursis	tu surseoiras
il sursoit	il sursoyait	il sursit	il surseoira
nous sursoyons	nous sursoyions	nous sursîmes	nous surseoirons
vous sursoyez	vous sursoyiez	vous sursîtes	vous surseoirez
ils sursoient	ils sursoyaient	ils sursirent	ils surseoiront

Passé composé: j'ai sursis . . . elle a sursis, *she delayed, she has delayed.*

Participe présent: sursoyant, *delaying.*

Conditionnel *I would delay*	**Impératif** *delay*	**Prés. du subj.** *that I delay*	**Imparf. du subj.** *that I delayed*
je surseoirais		que je sursoie	que je sursisse
tu surseoirais	sursois	que tu sursoies	que tu sursisses
il surseoirait		qu'il sursoie	qu'il sursît
nous surseoirions	sursoyons	que n. sursoyions	que n. sursissions
vous surseoiriez	sursoyez	que v. sursoyiez	que v. sursissiez
ils surseoiraient		qu'ils sursoient	qu'ils sursissent

**TENIR, *to hold*

Prés. de l'ind. *I hold*	**Imparfait** *I was holding*	**Passé simple** *I held*	**Futur simple** *I will hold*
je tiens	je tenais	je tins	je tiendrai
tu tiens	tu tenais	tu tins	tu tiendras
il tient	il tenait	il tint	il tiendra
nous tenons	nous tenions	nous tînmes	nous tiendrons
vous tenez	vous teniez	vous tîntes	vous tiendrez
ils tiennent	ils tenaient	ils tinrent	ils tiendront

Passé composé: j'ai tenu . . . elle a tenu, *she held, she has held.*			
Participe présent: tenant, *holding.*			
Conditionnel *I would hold* je tiendrais tu tiendrais il tiendrait nous tiendrions vous tiendriez ils tiendraient	**Impératif** *hold* tiens tenons tenez	**Prés. du subj.** *that I hold* que je tienne que tu tiennes qu'il tienne que n. tenions que v. teniez qu'ils tiennent	**Imparf. du subj.** *that I held* que je tinsse que tu tinsses qu'il tînt que n. tinssions que v. tinssiez qu'ils tinssent

Conjugated like **tenir** are: **s'abstenir** *(with* **être)**, *to abstain, to refrain from;* ***appartenir,** *to belong;* **contenir,** *to contain;* **détenir,** *to be in possession of, to detain;* ***entretenir,** *to maintain, to keep up;* ***maintenir,** *to maintain;* ***obtenir,** *to obtain;* ***retenir,** *to retain, to hold back;* ***soutenir,** *to support, to sustain, to prop up.*

TRAIRE, *to milk a cow*

Prés. de l'ind. *I milk* je trais tu trais il trait nous trayons vous trayez ils traient	**Imparfait** *I was milking* je trayais tu trayais il trayait nous trayions vous trayiez ils trayaient	**Passé simple**	**Futur simple** *I will milk* je trairai tu trairas il traira nous trairons vous trairez ils trairont
Passé composé: j'ai trait . . . elle a trait, *she milked, she has milked.*			
Participe présent: trayant, *milking.*			
Conditionnel *I would milk* je trairais tu trairais il trairait nous trairions vous trairiez ils trairaient	**Impératif** *milk* trais trayons trayez	**Prés. du subj.** *that I milk* que je traie que tu traies qu'il traie que n. trayions que v. trayiez qu'ils traient	**Imparf. du subj.**

Conjugated like **traire** are: **abstraire,** *to abstract, to separate;* **distraire,** *to divert (s.o's attention), to amuse, to entertain;* **extraire,** *to extract;* **soustraire,** *to take away, to substract.* **Braire,** *to bray,* is also conjugated like **traire,** but it is only used in the third persons of the Present Indicative, the Future and the Conditional.

*VAINCRE, *to vanquish, to conquer, to defeat*

Prés. de l'ind. *I defeat*		**Imparfait** *I was defeating*		**Passé simple** *I defeated*		**Futur simple** *I will defeat*	
je	vaincs	je	vainquais	je	vainquis	je	vaincrai
tu	vaincs	tu	vainquais	tu	vainquis	tu	vaincras
il	vainc	il	vainquait	il	vainquit	il	vaincra
nous	vainquons	nous	vainquions	nous	vainquîmes	nous	vaincrons
vous	vainquez	vous	vainquiez	vous	vainquîtes	vous	vaincrez
ils	vainquent	ils	vainquaient	ils	vainquirent	ils	vaincront

Passé composé: j'ai vaincu . . . elle a vaincu, *she defeated, she has defeated.*

Participe présent: vainquant, *defeating.*

Conditionnel *I should defeat*		**Impératif** *defeat*	**Prés. du subj.** *that I defeat*		**Imparf. du subj.** *that I defeated*	
je	vaincrais		que je	vainque	que je	vainquisse
tu	vaincrais	vaincs	que tu	vainques	que tu	vainquisses
il	vaincrait		qu'il	vainque	qu'il	vainquît
nous	vaincrions	vainquons	que n.	vainquions	que n.	vainquissions
vous	vaincriez	vainquez	que v.	vainquiez	que v.	vainquissiez
ils	vaincraient		qu'ils	vainquent	qu'ils	vainquissent

Convaincre, *to convince,* is conjugated like **vaincre.**

*VALOIR, *to be worth, to deserve, to bring in*

Prés. de l'ind. *I deserve*		**Imparfait** *I was deserving*		**Passé simple** *I deserved*		**Futur simple** *I will deserve*	
je	vaux	je	valais	je	valus	je	vaudrai
tu	vaux	tu	valais	tu	valus	tu	vaudras
il	vaut	il	valait	il	valut	il	vaudra
nous	valons	nous	valions	nous	valûmes	nous	vaudrons
vous	valez	vous	valiez	vous	valûtes	vous	vaudrez
ils	valent	ils	valaient	ils	valurent	ils	vaudront

Passé composé: j'ai valu . . . elle a valu, *she deserved, she has deserved.*

Participe présent: valant, *deserving.*

Conditionnel *I would deserve*		**Impératif** *deserve*	**Prés. du subj.** *that I deserve*		**Imparf. du subj.** *that I deserved*	
je	vaudrais		que je	vaille	que je	valusse
tu	vaudrais	vaux	que tu	vailles	que tu	valusses
il	vaudrait		qu'il	vaille	qu'il	valût
nous	vaudrions	valons	que n.	valions	que n.	valussions
vous	vaudriez	valez	que v.	valiez	que v.	valussiez
ils	vaudraient		qu'ils	vaillent	qu'ils	valussent

Conjugated like **valoir** are: **équivaloir,** *to be equal in value;* **prévaloir** (except in the Present Subjunctive, **que je prévale,** etc.) *to prevail;* **revaloir,** *to return, to pay back.*

**VENIR, *to come*

Prés. de l'ind. *I come*	**Imparfait** *I was coming*	**Passé simple** *I came*	**Futur simple** *I will come*
je viens	je venais	je vins	je viendrai
tu viens	tu venais	tu vins	tu viendras
il vient	il venait	il vint	il viendra
nous venons	nous venions	nous vînmes	nous viendrons
vous venez	vous veniez	vous vîntes	vous viendrez
ils viennent	ils venaient	ils vinrent	ils viendront

Passé composé: je suis venu . . . elle est venue, *she came, she has come.*

Participe présent: venant, *coming.*

Conditionnel *I would come*	**Impératif** *come*	**Prés. du subj.** *that I come*	**Imparf. du subj.** *that I came*
je viendrais		que je vienne	que je vinsse
tu viendrais	viens	que tu viennes	que tu vinsses
il viendrait		qu'il vienne	qu'il vînt
nous viendrions	venons	que n. venions	que n. vinssions
vous viendriez	venez	que v. veniez	que v. vinssiez
ils viendraient		qu'ils viennent	qu'ils vinssent

Conjugated like **venir** are: ***devenir,** *to become;* ***intervenir,** *to intervene;* ***parvenir,** *to arrive at, to reach (a place), to succeed;* ***provenir,** *to proceed, to result, to arise;* **redevenir,** *to become again;* **se ressouvenir,** *to remember (again);* ***revenir,** *to return, to come back;* **se souvenir,** *to remember;* **survenir,** *to happen, to arrive unexpectedly.*
Also conjugated like **venir** but using the auxiliary **avoir** in their compound tenses are: **circonvenir (j'ai circonvenu,** etc.), *to outwit;* **contrevenir,** *to contravene, to infringe (an order);* **disconvenir,** *to be unsuitable for, not to agree;* ***prévenir,** *to anticipate, to forewarn;* **subvenir,** *to provide for the needs of s.o.* ***Convenir,** conjugated like **venir**, is conjugated with **être** to emphasize a state and with **avoir** to emphasize the action: **ils sont convenus de céder,** *they are agreed to give in* , **ils ont convenu de le congédier,** *they agreed to sack him.*

VÊTIR, *to dress, to clothe, to put on (garment)*

Prés. de l'ind. *I dress*	**Imparfait** *I was dressing*	**Passé simple** *I dressed*	**Futur simple** *I will dress*
je vêts	je vêtais	je vêtis	je vêtirai
tu vêts	tu vêtais	tu vêtis	tu vêtiras
il vêt	il vêtait	il vêtit	ils vêtira
nous vêtons	nous vêtions	nous vêtîmes	nous vêtirons
vous vêtez	vous vêtiez	vous vêtîtes	vous vêtirez
ils vêtent	ils vêtaient	ils vêtirent	ils vêtiront

Passé composé: j'ai vêtu . . . elle a vêtu, *she dressed, she has dressed.*

Participe présent: vêtant, dressing.

Conditionnel *I would dress*	Impératif *dress*	Prés. du subj. *that I dress*	Imparf. du subj. *that I dressed*
je vêtirais		que je vête	que je vêtisse
tu vêtirais	vêts	que tu vêtes	que tu vêtisses
il vêtirait		qu'il vête	qu'il vêtît
nous vêtirions	vêtons	que n. vêtions	que n. vêtissions
vous vêtiriez	vêtez	que v. vêtiez	que v. vêtissiez
ils vêtiraient		qu'ils vêtent	qu'ils vêtissent

Conjugated like **vêtir** are: **dévêtir,** *to undress,* and **revêtir,** *to reclothe, to dress, to put on.*

N.B. Many authors conjugate **vêtir** in many tenses like **finir,** e.g. **il vêtit** instead of **il vêt; ils vêtissaient** instead of **ils vêtaient.**

**VIVRE, *to live*

Prés. de l'ind. *I live*	Imparfait *I was living*	Passé simple *I lived*	Futur simple *I will live*
je vis	je vivais	je vécus	je vivrai
tu vis	tu vivais	tu vécus	tu vivras
il vit	il vivait	il vécut	il vivra
nous vivons	nous vivions	nous vécûmes	nous vivrons
vous vivez	vous viviez	vous vécûtes	vous vivrez
ils vivent	ils vivaient	ils vécurent	ils vivront

Passé composé: j'ai vécu . . . elle a vécu, *she lived, she has lived.*

Participe présent: vivant, *living.*

Conditionnel *I would live*	Impératif *live*	Prés. du subj. *that I live*	Imparf. du subj. *that I lived*
je vivrais		que je vive	que je vécusse
tu vivrais	vis	que tu vives	que tu vécusses
il vivrait		qu'il vive	qu'il vécût
nous vivrions	vivons	que n. vivions	que n. vécussions
vous vivriez	vivez	que v. viviez	que v. vécussiez
ils vivraient		qu'ils vivent	qu'ils vécussent

Conjugated like **vivre** are: **revivre,** *to live again, to come to life again,* and **survivre,** *to survive.*

**VOIR, *to see*

Prés. de l'ind. *I see*	**Imparfait** *I was seeing*	**Passé simple** *I saw*	**Futur simple** *I will see*
je vois	je voyais	je vis	je verrai
tu vois	tu voyais	tu vis	tu verras
il voit	il voyait	il vit	il verra
nous voyons	nous voyions	nous vîmes	nous verrons
vous voyez	vous voyiez	vous vîtes	vous verrez
ils voient	ils voyaient	ils virent	ils verront

Passé composé: j'ai vu . . . elle a vu, *she saw, she has seen.*

Participe présent: voyant, *seeing.*

Conditionnel *I would see*	**Impératif** *see*	**Prés. du subj.** *that I see*	**Imparf. du subj.** *that I saw*
je verrais		que je voie	que je visse
tu verrais	vois	que tu voies	que tu visses
il verrait		qu'il voie	qu'il vît
nous verrions	voyons	que n. voyions	que n. vissions
vous verriez	voyez	que v. voyiez	que v. vissiez
ils verraient		qu'ils voient	qu'ils vissent

Conjugated like **voir** are: **entrevoir,** *to catch a glimpse of;* ***revoir,** *to see again, to meet again;* ***prévoir,** *to foresee.* However **prévoir** in the Future and the Conditional is **je prévoirai . . . je prévoirais.** For **pourvoir** see page 44.

**VOULOIR, *to will, to be determined on, to want, to wish, to demand*

Prés. de l'ind. *I want*	**Imparfait** *I wanted*	**Passé simple** *I wanted*	**Futur simple** *I will want*
je veux	je voulais	je voulus	je voudrai
tu veux	tu voulais	tu voulus	tu voudras
il veut	il voulait	il voulut	il voudra
nous voulons	nous voulions	nous voulûmes	nous voudrons
vous voulez	vous vouliez	vous voulûtes	vous voudrez
ils veulent	ils voulaient	ils voulurent	ils voudront

Passé composé: j'ai voulu . . . elle a voulu, *she wanted, she has wanted.*

Participe présent: voulant, *wanting.*

Conditionnel *I would want*	**Impératif** *want*	**Prés. du subj.** *that I want*	**Imparf. du subj.** *that I wanted*
je voudrais		que je veuille	que je voulusse
tu voudrais	veux (veuille)	que tu veuilles	que tu voulusses
il voudrait		qu'il veuille	qu'il voulût
nous voudrions	voulons	que n. voulions	que n. voulussions
vous voudriez	voulez (veuillez)	que v. vouliez	que v. voulussiez
ils voudraient		qu'ils veuillent	qu'ils voulussent

* abaisser, *conj. like donner* 11
* s'abaisser
* abandonner, *like donner* 11
* abattre, *like battre* 23
* s'abattre
* abîmer, *like donner* 11
* aboutir, *like finir* 12
* abriter, *like donner* 11
* s'abriter
absoudre, *like résoudre* 46
s'abstenir, *like tenir* 50
abstraire, *like traire* 51
* accepter, *like donner* 11
* accompagner, *like donner* 11
* accomplir, *like finir* 12
* s'accomplir
* accorder, *like donner* 11
* s'accorder
* accourir, *like courir* 27
accroître, *like croître* 29
* accueillir, *like cueillir* 29
* accuser, *like donner* 11
* acheter, *like lever* 18
acquérir 21
* adapter, *like donner* 11
adjoindre, *like joindre* 37
* admettre, *like mettre* 38
* adopter, *like donner* 11
* adresser, *like donner* 11
* s'adresser
* affirmer, *like donner* 11
* agir, *like finir* 12
* s'agir de
* agiter, *like donner* 11
* s'agiter
* agréer, *like donner* 11
* aider, *like donner* 11
* aimer, *like donner* 11
* ajouter, *like donner* 11
** **aller** 21
* s'en aller
* allumer, *like donner* 11
* améliorer, *like donner* 11
* s'améliorer
* amener, *like lever* 18
* amuser, *like donner* 11
* annoncer, *like placer* 16
* apercevoir, *like recevoir* 46
* s'apercevoir,
* apparaître, *like connaître* 26
* appartenir, *like tenir* 50
** **appeler** 20
* s'appeler
* appliquer, *like donner* 11
* s'appliquer
* apporter, *like donner* 11
* apprécier, *like donner* 11
* apprendre, *like prendre* 45
* approcher, *like donner* 11
* s'approcher
* approuver, *like donner* 11
* appuyer, *like nettoyer* 17
* s'appuyer
* arracher, *like donner* 11
* arranger, *like manger* 16
* s'arranger
* arrêter, *like donner* 11
* s'arrêter
* arriver, *like monter* 14
* arroser, *like donner* 11
assaillir 22
asseoir 22
** **s'asseoir** 22
asservir, *like finir* 12
* assister, *like donner* 11
* associer, *like donner* 11
* s'associer
* assurer, *like donner* 11
* s'assurer
astreindre, *like peindre* 43
* attacher, *like donner* 11
* attaquer, *like donner* 11
* s'attaquer
* atteindre, *like peindre* 43
* attendre, *like vendre* 13
* attirer, *like donner* 11
* attraper, *like donner* 11
* augmenter, *like donner* 11
* autoriser, *like donner* 11
* avaler, *like donner* 11
* avancer, *like placer* 16
** **avoir** 23
* avouer, *like donner* 11

* baisser, *like donner* 11
* se baisser
* balayer, *like payer* 18
* bâtir, *like finir* 12
** **battre** 23
* se battre
* bénéficier, *like donner* 11
* blesser, *like donner* 11

*(a)*See p. 5, no. 3

(a) See p. 5, no. 3

(a) See p. 5, no. 3

(a) See p. 5, no. 3